Love Signs 1995

Aquarius

For a further insight into what the future holds for you, CALL THE SUNDAY EXPRESS ASTROLOGY LINES NOW:

The Secret of the Runes – see if the ancient spiritual tradition of the Rune Stones can answer your questions: **0891-111-666**

The Vision of the Cards – the 53 cards tell your fortune. Let us reveal their magic and see what the secret symbols of knowledge may hold in store for you: **0891-111-667**

Calls cost 39p per minute cheap rate, 49p per minute at all other times – prices correct at time of going to press

Sunday
EXPRESS

Love Signs 1995
Aquarius

21 January – 19 February

ARROW

First published in 1994

1 3 5 7 9 8 6 4 2

First published in the United Kingdom in 1994
by Vermilion Arrow
an imprint of Ebury Press
Random House, 20 Vauxhall Bridge Road,
London SW1V 2SA

Random House Australia (Pty) Limited
20 Alfred Street, Milsons Point, Sydney,
New South Wales 2061, Australia

Random House New Zealand Limited
18 Poland Road, Glenfield,
Auckland 10, New Zealand

Random House South Africa (Pty) Limited
PO Box 337, Bergvlei, 2012 South Africa

Random House UK Limited Reg. No. 954009

A CIP record for this title is available from the British Library

ISBN 009936851X

Designed by Nigel Hazle
Typeset from author's disks by Clive Dorman & Co.
Printed and bound in Great Britain by
Cox & Wyman Ltd, Reading, Berks

Contents

Introduction

**Astrology is about *how* we are,
not *why* we are.**

This book aims to be a guide to what you might expect from people as lovers, partners and friends. It also gives you an insight into who you really are, and how others see you. The forecasts for October 1994 through to December 1995 reveal the *mood* of the month for your Sun sign in the areas of love, emotions, sex, leisure and friendship. It will give you a fresh insight into getting the best out of your relationships for the months ahead. Keep your eyes on the stars and the stars in your eyes, and you won't go far wrong.

Astrology makes no claims to prophecy. It is only a reflection of human psychology: a mirror of us all and the paths we take.

Sun signs divide and generalise, no more or less than any other approach to our existence. They do show the basic qualities we have in common, the emotions and feelings and intellect that we all share and how we use our personal map of life. The map of life is in all of us, and every individual has his or her unique chart. Some areas of our personality are more prominent than others, like on the map of the world, where oceans and continents can be highlighted, or mountains or rivers. Sometimes we project different continents on to that map, other countries of feeling or mentality that are not highlighted on our own personal chart, but are highlighted in someone else.

There are so many other points involved in your natal chart that make you unique, so that when you read this book, remember that talking about a Virgo or a Scorpio can only be a beginning to knowing someone, the larger continents and oceans on their own psychological globe. These reactions and characteristics are not the only way a person will respond to situations. But Sun signs give guidance to the general way we feel, love and interact.

Unless your lover's Sun sign is severely afflicted, or has another more prominent sign in the natal chart, then he or she should be fairly consistent with the Sun sign image, though you may not recognise it instantly.

The sign rising over the horizon at the moment of birth has an equally powerful bearing on our psychological make-up. However, finding this out requires exact and detailed calculations, including certainty of time of birth. That is why our Sun sign is our primary pin-pointer on the map. You may not at first glance recognise yourself, because often your Sun sign reveals characteristics to which you don't want to admit!

As La Rochefoucauld put it so succinctly, 'Not all those who know their minds, know their hearts as well.'

The 12 Signs as Lovers and Partners

THE ARIES MAN

Aries is traditionally the first sign of the zodiac and that means that an Aries man comes first in everything. The Arien lover is bold, demanding, impulsive, and most certainly self-centred, and yet he will take risks in his relationships and in love. Because he cannot stand any kind of restriction to his freedom, you're more likely to find him hanging around motor races, rallies, outdoor activities rather than cutting cigar ends down the local pub. He's looking for adventure and, for the egotistic Ram, love-affairs are as much a challenge to him as hang-gliding.

One of the things that make him an exciting lover is his need to take chances. Romance to this impetuous man involves dragging you round the Himalayas at breathtaking speed and expecting you to eat vindaloo for lunch and dinner when you get back to the local Indian restaurant. He expects weekends in the camper in freezing winter with only each other to keep you warm! He needs a woman with guts both spirited and physically non-combustible to keep up with his vigorous lifestyle.

The arrogant Ram can fall in love easily, and impulsively, and if he genuinely believes that you are the answer to his dreams, he won't hesitate to become deeply involved. His sexual magnetism is tremendous, and he is so aware of his ability to attract women that he sometimes assumes that no one will reject him. This kind of arrogance can lead him into trouble, but his honest, no-nonsense approach always gets him back on top and he doesn't suffer from self-pity, ever.

What you must remember is that Arien hotheads are jealous Fire signs. It's quite all right for him to chat to other women, or even play a touch of harmless flirting, but for you to attempt even a smile at that charming colleague of his across the pub is fatal. In a crowded room you'll know the Aries man because he's the one with the self-confidence and the smile of a dare-devil lover. He might hastily introduce himself, arrogance and impulse working overtime to meet his challenger head-on. But if you crash, watch out for his honest vent to his feelings. It takes a lot to rile an Aries but, if you don't play fair and true, he won't let you forget it.

If you want a permanent relationship with him and can keep up with his energetic sex life you will be rewarded. But never forget that the Ram's egotism governs his need to satisfy himself first, and you second. But if you both can get over his self-centred approach to love and sex, for really he's always searching for an ideal, there is a lot of warmth and honest love waiting in his heart.

THE ARIES WOMAN

The Aries woman usually will want to be the boss in everything, including her love life. Because she is a Cardinal Fire sign, she knows intuitively what she wants. Some Aries girls will come straight to the point and pick you up, if you don't make the first move! Like her male equivalent, an Aries girl has great sexual magnetism, and if you're strong enough to take her on, you'll realise why her hot-headed vanity works.

Undoubtedly she will want to take over your whole life if you fall in with her hard-headed approach to relationships. She will always be ambitious for you, and for where she comes in your life. She is number one, and you will always be number two. If you can bear her egotistic pride then she will be the most loving and passionate partner, but she needs commitment, and she needs to be the centre of your world, or she'll dump you.

Another important consideration is that exclusivity is her *raison d'être*. And that will mean you. Once she's let you into the secret art of ram-shearing then she can get incredibly jealous if you stray out of the sheep pen. She may be a passionate lover, but that passion doesn't make her liberal about free love.

The Ram girl likes men to be young in outlook and appearance. If you've got the energy to go hang-gliding before lunch then you'll be her friend for life. But if you've got a gut hanging out over your trousers and would rather sit in front of the TV with a can of lager, forget having any relationship with her. She needs an energetic man both as a friend, to make impulsive trips and exciting journeys, but also in bed. There is a fire burning in her soul which doesn't need to be put out, it just needs rekindling from time to time. The adventure in her head and the energy in her blood keep her restlessly searching for the next impulsive trip on love. Love is beautiful if she can be the boss, and she can take control, but give her back as much as she puts into a relationship and you'll stay her adventure for life.

THE TAURUS MAN

The natural inclination of Mr Bull at dawn is to force himself out of the bed he cherishes so much. But that's the only bit of forcing he'll do, particularly in any relationship. If he wants you then *you* have to be the one to chase him, but the move will be welcomed. A Taurean male won't actually make many advances and stubbornly waits for those who are worthy of his incredible sensual attention to come running.

For all this laid-back man-appeal it may appear that sex means little to him. But actually that's the catch. The Taurean male's quite seething sexuality, once unleashed on an unsuspecting female who decides to consider him as her partner, can be quite overtly bestial.

He thinks as highly of his body as he does of the next meal or the next bath. The Bull loves the pleasures and luxuries of life and is essentially an implacable part of the earth, intensely sensual, and dependable. He is an Earth sign whose energy and sexual drive originates from all that natural organic goodness that ironically he rarely eats.

There's actually something quite elusive about Taureans. You can never quite fathom out where they've come from, or really exactly where they are going to, probably because they really have no idea, nor care about it themselves. This is why it can take a long time to form a deep relationship with a Bull. If you do get past the horns, this affair could be for life. The placid Bull needs gentle handling, both emotionally and sexually. The trouble is that Mr Bull is often very blind to his own compatibility ratings. He is lured by, and hopelessly attracted to, Fire and Air signs. The Taurean man often gets tangled up with the Airy intellect or impulsive brainstorming of these very opposite types from him. He just can't keep up with the mind-bending improvisation that these signs so naturally use to charm their way through life.

The Taurus man is warm-hearted and affectionate, and he is intensely passionate. But he is a lover of the pleasures of life, a hedonist in every self-indulgence, and every luxury. Sex is a good, basic pleasure which he enjoys as part of a deep and erotic relationship. If after a heavy night of wining and dining he prefers to sleep off the last glass of brandy rather than spend the night with you, it's not that he's selfish, just that he forgot you for a while. After all, there are other sensual things in his life apart from sex, had you forgotten that?

THE TAURUS WOMAN

It's hard to imagine the placid, reliable, earth mother as a hard-edged Bull, but there is a side to her which might have been overlooked! A Taurean female takes a long time to decide if you are worthy of her passion, yet she has the power and the guts actually to initiate the first move in a relationship and should never be underestimated. A bossy girl needs careful handling, and because she is strong-minded and loyal she needs first-class devotion in return.

The Bull lady bears little resemblance to bovine sexuality except for an occasional grumbling temper and a geyser of bubbling anger when she gets overheated by resentment. Pouts grow on a female Taurean's lips very easily. Jealousy is uncommon, but possessiveness is. Her placid, controlled approach to your relationship is her self-protection, her magic eye. She has to impress and be impressed, which is why she often gets tangled up with men with a big cheque book. She likes the sound of champagne corks flying and the permanence of marriage.

Sensuality is the Taurean girl's be-all and end-all. It could be the summer rain pattering on your back as you kiss beneath an umbrella, or making love in the pine forest or beside the babbling stream. She's a creature of the outdoors, of closeness to nature and filling her senses with tastes, sounds and touch.

Venus in cowhide will be delighted equally whether she's having sex, floating in a silky warm ocean, eating pizzas at three in the morning, or cooking you both a cordon bleu breakfast in a tent. Sex is not to be taken lightly and she can get quite prudish with women who are apparent flirts or downright promiscuous. Convinced that a good emotional and sexual relationship is the answer to fulfilment, she might well confide her Mother Earth instincts to you one warm night.

The awkward and niggling little word 'possession' might create a spot of tension but, if you're willing to be a mate for life, or at least more permanent than the fading perfume on her skin, you will have to take sex and love as seriously as she does. If you can offer her honesty and maybe a sound financial future, a superb champagne dinner or a night listening to the owls in the woods, then she will be impressed enough to let you through her tough, resilient Bull-skin.

This girl needs both erotic and sensual communication, a man who can give her a down-to-earth lifestyle and a really warm heart. But make sure you've got the stamina and nerve to accept her blatant honesty if she decides to reject you!

THE GEMINI MAN

The highly versatile, spontaneous and amusing Gemini man is always ready for any mental and sexual challenge. He lives in the air, rather than flat-footed on the ground. Passion and sensuality are a rarity in his love life, for he is the catalyst of communication. The will o' the wisp is inquisitive, and like a child he will want to play games, will move through your life like a shooting star, and never make promises about tomorrow. He is privileged with a youthful appearance and a youthful approach to life. But emotionally, Gemini men rarely let you into their space, in fact they can often seem very cold, in the air, out of their heads and hardly ever in their hearts.

The second problem with which you have to wrestle is that there are always at least two personalities to cope with in one guise. This can be quite alarming when you wake up in the morning with a total stranger, not the man you thought you spent the night with! The seductive and alluring man of the late evening can turn into the clown at breakfast, and never be prepared to stay for lunch. The cherub-like Botticelli twins are actually not so much twins as a couple of conmen, both trying to outwit the other. Because of the mental struggle of trying to figure out his own identity, a Gemini male needs variety and change in his life. This means that he is often promiscuous, often marries at least twice and always wants two of everything. He has this uncanny ability and agility to be all types of lovers imaginable because role-playing stops him from ever being truly himself. And actually he really doesn't know who he is himself.

The double-lover enjoys the company and friendship of females just as much as any intimate physical relationship. Sexually he is the least chauvinistic of the star signs, and would rather spend the evening discussing the world and sipping champagne with you than be down the pub with the boys. He prefers to move on, to change partners, to try out new experiences, whatever forecast is in the wind, and to leave the fog of commitment and emotion far behind him.

If you can give him fun and variety he might even hang around to breathe your kind of fresh air. The Gemini man is often likened to Peter Pan, but if you ask any girl who's been involved with the Twins, she'll say, 'Sure, he reminded me of Peter Pan; but wasn't he like all those lost boys too?'.

THE GEMINI WOMAN

The female twins sparkle at parties, vibrating among other women who would rather keep cool and mysterious and watch this flirting charmer draw men to her like junkies to a fix. That's why a distortion of the facts has arisen and Miss Gemini has been dubbed two-faced in love, and a hypocrite in bed. So it's about time the true nature of this multi-faceted woman was revealed!

They seek out and need constant change in both their social lives and their love lives, not to mention their careers and their home life. Miss Fickle can jump headlong from the trivial to the profound in a split second because she's more interested in actual cleverness than the truth. She may have two or more faces, but they are all *genuine* in her own eyes, and in her own pretty head. Gemini girls are adept at role-playing, from switching from heaven to earth. Give them a character, a *femme fatale*, an innocent virgin, a career woman, you name it, they can play it. If you can keep up with their flighty, pacey, restless way of life, then you'll have more than one woman to keep you company at bedtime.

Apart from the thousand faces that Gemini women possess they are also known to be incredible flirts. It's not so much that she's particularly infatuated with you, it's more likely that she wants to play the game, drink her way through a bottle of champagne and then go home to sleep off the mental exhaustion of it all. She needs a lot of sleep, but a Gemini woman is more likely than any other sign to prefer to sit up all night discussing the latest philosophy, or the latest painting in your collection, or the books on your shelf.

She makes vague attachments, and loves socialising, but very rarely makes deep friendships, particularly with her own sex. Miss Fickle prefers the company of men to women and would rather be one of the boys at the office.

Gregarious girls meet a lot of blokes, so Gemini woman will be well surrounded by a choice selection. But remember, she's attracted to appearances rather than to depth of emotions. She is capable of persuading herself you're the love of her life. Being in love is easy if you talk yourself into it. Why, then, you can talk yourself out of it again when it takes your fancy, or another man does! (By the way, a Gemini girl's heart is a pretty cold place to penetrate, but if you ever get through the surface with your ice-pick at least you take pleasure in knowing that you will be remembered in her heart for being the only man that ever made it!)

The Jekyll girl often has affairs with younger men because she feels safer; commitment won't be spread across the bed with the Sunday papers at eleven in the morning after a night of hot passion. The marmalade men, the electric shavers and the city bods who need slippers and pipe won't attract her. She is capable of finding something fascinating and appealing in practically all men, but that doesn't mean it will last more than the second that it takes for her to change their mind, instantly! Enjoying sex isn't the answer to her dreams, only another dream can have that solution. And you can't stay her dream for ever – or can you?

THE CANCER MAN

The Cancerian man is home-loving, gentle and sincere. He responds deeply to life and to every change in emotion or feelings around him. His goodness far excels his weaker, depressive side which can get unbearable and drown an affair in melancholy. His moods can be touchy, he can be as snappy as an alligator and he takes everything too personally, fearing rejection. Yet on the surface he will play the extrovert, be flirtatious, the lunatic everyone loves at the all-night party.

A Crab man is overtly sentimental. He will take a long time to pluck up enough courage to phone you, until he is sure in his Crab-like way he can move in for love. Don't forget, Crabs move sideways, stay in their shells and guard themselves ferociously with giant claws.

He might seem mildly indifferent: playing guessing games about his true motives with you when he first takes you out to dinner.

He loves food, and if you offer him breakfast in bed he might just agree to scrambling the eggs himself. This man needs smothering with affection, and sexually can be languid and lazy when it suits him, especially once he feels secure in a relationship. Typical of Water signs, he feeds on gentle rhythms, quiet arousal and delicate love-making.

Don't ever mention your past boyfriends because he will see vivid mental movies about where you have been, and who you have been with. Cancerians are very possessive, and if you mention ex-partners, he will wallow in self-pity for days.

Don't ever look at anyone once you're married. You are collected, part of his acquisitions and his very personal private collection.

Cancer men hide out in the dark corners of pubs, or at the edge of the in-crowd. If they use their extrovert shell to cover up their weaker personality they can be awkward to spot. Sometimes they hover in the wings, hiding from possible failure, appearing as confident and glib as any fire sign. But around the full moon you can usually spot them when they become touchy and moody, not at all like any Fire sign!

The Crab is easily flattered, and often gullible in the face of a strong protective, woman. He has a cheeky, little-boy-lost appeal that he takes to parties in his search for the perfect soul-mate, and he needs one desperately for all his apparent self-confidence and arrogant manner. It's misleading. Beneath that gregarious shell is a soft heart. There will only ever be one woman at a time for a Cancerian man – at least you can be assured of that.

THE CANCER WOMAN

When you meet the Cancer woman you will immediately know that you have met the most female of all females. The Yin is intense, explosive, warm and genuine, the genie of the zodiac, the sensitive soul, the Moon disabled by love and emotion. You have nothing to fear, except yourself, and the changeability of her deep and dark side. The dark side of the Moon waits for you. Do not disappoint her for the woman with whom you have just become infatuated is the past-mistress of love and romance.

Cancer ladies are easily flattered and at their worst are unstable. Preparation for a life of swaying moods, indistinct emotions and powerful sensitivity have adapted this dippy bird to seek attention and seek out sympathy from a nice guy, one she hopes will have a larger cheque book than her own.

She is protective, gentle, highly intuitive and reflective of others' moods. Yet like the Moon she sways, changing the light of the night from that pale ghostly shadowland to human and loony laughter. A bit touched, a bit sad, occasionally glad, Moon birds need close friends, domesticity and a strong, tender man to support them.

You can only get so close to a Moon bird. She has this intense fear of being opened up like a clam. The big problem for her is that if she doesn't open up then you might reject her like the bad mussels in the cooking pot that get tossed in the bin. Frankly, the Cancerian girl needs a permanent, stable relationship with someone who won't get twisted and confused every time she sulks or goes loopy in the Full Moon. You've been introduced to an apparently hard, tough, thick-skinned woman in the crowd. It really seems unlikely that someone so extrovert and resilient could be reduced to tears by a slight put-down. But she can! She's an extrovert/introvert, a manic depressive and a bundle of fun when she's on one of her highs. She can be downright rude and criticise everything about you from your haircut to your taste in underwear but she won't survive an in-depth dissection of her own deeper and often weaker character. Cancer women will never make the first move, because they sincerely cannot cope with rejection.

A word of warning. This lady can get her claws into you quicker and more deviously than any other Crab this side of the Moon. The claws of a Crab can grab you and, pincer-like, they'll clutch at your heart and possessively monopolise you, as she possesses her books, her kitchen memorabilia and her dog.

Her imagination sizzles in bed, like throwing water on fire. But she needs emotional and sensual fulfilment, a physical experience that will change as easily as her moods. Cancerian ladies don't take to athletic body-building, or get obsessed about their weight, but they will make or break the sexual traditions if it means pleasing the one man they really want to impress.

THE LEO MAN

The Leo man is known for his magnanimous nature and his warm and generous heart. But he is also a prowler, one of the more sexually active signs of the zodiac. Like Capricorn and Scorpio he is motivated by power. The subtle difference is that Leo assumes success in everything he does, particularly when it involves relationships and love. He can't bear the thought of rejection so he never even thinks about it. That's why he blazes his way through life, and that is how he wins.

For all his flash behaviour the tom-cat is actually in need of a lot of stroking. He falls in love easily, but it will often be subconsciously motivated by the desire to impress whoever he is with. The Cat is a show-cat, wherever and his companion. Leos have dramatic tastes, extrovert and extravagant desires, unnerving energy and yet he is so self-opinionated that he can be intolerably conceited and inflexible.

They need to be in the headlines and to draw attention to themselves, so the Leo lover will look for the sort of woman who can enhance his Mogul image and taste for hedonistic delights.

If you're good-looking, independent, can hold your own and be part of his show, then he'll fall in love with you on sight. The one thing you have to remember is that the golden boy, for all his showiness, is actually not very brave. He doesn't take risks like an Arien or Sagittarian, and he generally takes more care about who he gets involved with to avoid hurting his delicate pride. His emotions are fiery, but his judgment is cautious.

For long-term commitment, a Leo will be willing to take the risk only if he gets as much attention as he believes he deserves.

He will have mastered all the techniques of high performance love-making. That is something that he can really impress you with. But while you're enthralled by his energetic love and sexuality, remember that he likes to play the Tom-and-Jerry game. Mostly he prefers to be Tom, but even Tom needs a lot of affection and warmth, for all his boasting conceit. Cold, unresponsive girls can make him temporarily impotent and turn that organised high-flyer to anger; and that's when he can really leave a trail of charred hearts!

THE LEO WOMAN

The Cat woman is one of those girls who is always surrounded by men at social events. She will insist on being the centre of attention at all parties, which is one of the reasons she always organises them. The Leo girl also assumes she will be the nucleus and hotbed in any relationship and, for her, relationships need to be warm, affectionate and full of physical expressions of love. Bear-hugs, stroking her wild hair as if she is a pussy-cat are all gestures that show how she is adored. And she needs that very badly. This naturally vivacious, clever Cat finds men drawn to her like mosquitoes to blood.

This very sexual Cat can at times be overpowering and overdramatic, but her magnetic personality always catches the limelight.

Leo was born to lead, and not to follow. If you are strong enough to challenge her, then she may play the role of a sweet innocent for a while. But if she's not the starring role in your life then the loud, extravagant will of her ego will come hurtling out to confront you. And a Leo in full temper and voice is a pretty frightening Big Cat!

Her vanity irritates other women and attracts many men, and she can be arrogant and incredibly stubborn. She is self-opinionated, but she is also generous and compassionate, able to create the kind of atmosphere in the bedroom fit for the most sensual and seductive love-making imaginable!

If you can keep up with her energy and delight in passionate and exciting sex, then she might decide to make you a permanent fixture. The Cat woman will scratch for her independence, and won't sacrifice her career or freedom for many men. Although she will flirt her way through a boardroom of old fogeys to assure success in her career, you will have to trust her integrity.

Flatter her and she'll let you closer. Her vanity and her magnetic personality are, ironically, her weakness. But with respect and belief in a Leo woman you can be assured of a loyal and true partner. Never try to control her or play ego games. She needs a strong man who will pamper her; give her the world and in return she'll give you everything back. Attention-getting, and attention-seeking go together, so be prepared for the occasional mild flirtations when she's out at her business lunches, or career parties. If she weren't the star of the show someone else would be, and she really doesn't want anyone else to take that leading part away from her.

THE VIRGO MAN

If anyone could be more accurate, more perfect at time-keeping than a quartz watch, then it would have to be the Virgo man. He is the precision master, the careful and discriminating quiet one in the corner of the bar, who will drink exactly the same amount of alcohol every visit, and who knows precisely the health advantages of wine and the mortality rate of heavy drinkers. This neat and tidy man often pulls weights down the gym rather than girls, and worries about his digestion and whether he should be celibate.

The Virgo man finds warm, emotional relationships difficult, and yet he seeks out quality and the perfect woman. He analyses sex and relationships with the meticulous interest of a stamp-collector. You see, Virgo men don't really need anyone else in their lives. They often panic about their lack of passion, and then devote an awful lot of time worrying about it. (Virgos are constantly fretting about life.) Mr Precision sometimes falls in love with the logic of a relationship, with the actual methodology of it all, but very rarely is deep and genuine emotion involved.

Virgo men have this thing about purity. Not that they are chaste and virginal, but they will search for the purist form of experience and will often sublimate passion for neutrality. This is why if you're not near perfect in his eyes you'll be rejected before he even attempts to test you out. Sex can be a pure and impeccable experience for a Virgo with a girl in mint condition and the right motivation. But is there any life in his soul, any passion or warmth in that apparent cold and solitary physique?

He is very attractive to women because he appears to be a challenge. If you get past that cold shoulder there might just be a sensual, sensational warm heart. He has a heart, but it's as invulnerable as his emotions. On the surface he is the perfect lover and can perform like Don Juan. He is the sexual technocrat of the zodiac. If you can put up with his dissection of your personality, if you like a distant lover and a punctual friend, a lover who is dextrous but unemotional, he might make one of the better permanent relationships. But he compartmentalises life: the past stays the past, the future the future. He carries little sentimental or emotional baggage with him. It's tidier, isn't it?

If you finally get through the cold earth that buries this man you'll find a faithful lover. He's not exactly a bundle of laughs, but the strong silent type who once he's found his perfect partner will never, ever look at another woman again.

THE VIRGO WOMAN

The Virgo girl is quiet, self-aware and keeps her eyes firmly pinned on anything that might remotely interfere with her calculated plans for life. This includes her personal relationships which are as critically analysed and subjected to meticulous scrutiny as if she were conducting a witch hunt or a scientific experiment.

Miss Virgo is not only critical of herself, she is acutely critical of others. She nit-picks rather than knits, and can really infuriate you with her constant reminder that you have a speck of dandruff, or your tie is wonky. She believes that she knows best, and this confident mental sharpness affects all her personal and sexual relationships.

She expects tidiness and perfection around her which includes an organised pristine relationship with her ideal man. The Virgo girl can lack real human warmth at her worst and, because she is such a worrier, even sex can become a chore, and your performance tainted with imaginary faults.

But a Virgo girl loves romance: the first innocent kiss or the love-letters scribbled from a stranger. She can become infatuated with someone over the phone, or by the pure physical beauty in a man. She loves sentiment and delicate love-making. An Interflora sign will make her weep and she's nuts about soppy films, as long as no one is with her when she watches them. If you are too dominant a partner she can become frigid just to suit herself. Coldness is natural to her.

Perfection is wasted on talentless men and she will often be fatally attracted to opposite dreamy types, escapist musicians and artists who, although they fulfil her romantic fantasy, lead her to find fault with every work of art or creation they perform. The Virgo girl is dedicated to pursuing happiness, and her strength is to be able to be both obsessively practical and ridiculously romantic, because love is the purist form of analysis.

Sex will be a delight to her if you keep it light and

emotionless, but don't ever be late for a date, or her time-keeping will start clocking you in and out of her bed. She'll never be unfaithful, it's not in her nature. But if you can't enflame that spark of sexuality out of her ice-box she will quite coldly and mercilessly look for it elsewhere. The modest, clever and cautious Virgo girl will be the most affectionate and prudent partner if you can accept her perfectionism. She might decide you're her ideal and throw a party; but she'll stay in the kitchen and worry about the spilled punch. Someone has to haven't they?

THE LIBRA MAN

Libra is the go-between of the zodiac – the man who can be active or passive, will be laid-back, indecisive and fluctuate between love and sex in his head, easy-going, well mannered and everybody's friend. Doesn't that sound like the sort of man you would love to have around? Someone with wit and humour, who curves through life rather than angles through it? He is essentially a relaxed man who is fair and lovely about the world and naturally charming with every female he meets.

He needs harmony, beauty and idealistic truth in his life. For him, life has to fulfil dreams of romance, particularly when love and sex are involved. But this is where he gets confused. Not because he's a soppy sentimentalist, far from it, but because he thinks sex is love and love is sex. You just can't have one without the other, it wouldn't be fair.

This sociable man needs and demands a lot of friends of both sexes. If you get involved with a Libra be prepared to tolerate all the other female friends he spoils. Some of them may even be ex-lovers that he hasn't quite decided whether to see again or not.

But there are times when a Libran won't be forced into making a decision at all and, when it comes to any conflict, emotional or physical, he would rather walk out than fight. The eternal problem for Librans is *not* making a decision. What bugs him is why he has to make a choice about commitment in his relationship, because essentially he hates to reject anything, and that mostly includes his freedom.

He wants the best of both worlds, if he can get it, and flirting his way through life enables him to meet many women, and maybe, just maybe, he'll find the girl of his dreams. He often gets led astray by strong, glamorous females. He can fall instantly in love, but he falls in love with the essence of the affair, rather than the girl. The face value of the romance is all that matters to him initially.

Like Gemini the Ping Pong man is attracted to the appearance of life, not any underlying spiritual meaning.

He's a romantic and a balloon-seller of ideals, releasing them on a windy day to see if they fly alone. He loves the romance of sex, the caresses, the body language, the first meetings. Sexually his head rules his body. His approach is one of airy, cloudless skies and often a languid, lazy love-making. But his soaring passion is an insubstantial mental process, and he often has trouble 'being there' with you.

This sexual egalitarian is a wonderful lover and romantic, but remember, he can fall out of love as easily as he fell into it!

THE LIBRA WOMAN

What if you meet a Libran woman surrounded by a group of adoring friends and she decided you were the most attractive, exciting man in the room? You invite her to dinner and she falls in love with your eyes and your hair and immediately and uncharacteristically accepts the date. An hour later the chances are she'll change her mind, or sweetly point out that actually she is with Tom, an old flame, and really she can't accept because they are already going down the pub that night. What if Tom got upset?

And what if Tom really was the man of her life, the ideal she's searching for? And then what if she rejects your offer and you don't make another? This is the terrible dilemma for a Libran woman.

She is lovely, perfectly lovely. Attractive, gregarious, articulate, spirited and independent. A real woman but with a tough head and a strong heart. She's mentally alert and logical about life like any Air sign, but she really hates to reject anything, or anyone. And making decisions just means not having the best of both worlds, doesn't it?

Libran women have deliberately charming smiles which they can turn on when it suits them, to show how wonderfully feminine they can be. But the logical intensity of her mental gymnastics can be slightly off-putting if your intentions are of a deeper or more physical need.

She needs honesty, beauty and truth around her, no heavy emotion and no remorse. She'll cheer you up when you're down, brighten your life with her sparkling humour and will thoroughly enjoy sexual pleasure and hedonistic delights. Don't be a spoilsport or a worm, and if you can't find your way out of a paper bag then you're not her kind of man.

She'll love you for ever if you are her mental equal and her physical mirror image. But remember, this girl can be led astray by beauty and by the idea of love. Like her male counterpart, she can fall in love with the affair before she knows who you are. She'll listen to your opinions about politics, point out her own, then with equal fairness spout everyone else's point of view. That's why getting close to her heart can take a long time. She talks a lot, and she talks for everyone. Can you really find her beneath all those fair judgments?

THE SCORPIO MAN

Apart from a snake or a hypnotist, a Scorpio man has the best chance of fixing his penetrating eyes upon the one he loves or lusts and capturing her. No matter how hard you resist if he gets it in his head to seduce you, this man will hypnotise you before you've got back from the bar with your glass of white wine.

Like any insect, the Scorpio male has the ability to rattle and repel. You can meet him at the standard office party and find him offensive and unnerving, disagree with him about every subject under the sun, but he'll have you, and there's nothing you can do about it!

In Yoga, Kundalini is the serpent who lives at the base of our spine and is awakened upon sexual arousal. Any true Scorpio male's Kundalini is on permanent red-alert. To him sex and love are the whole meaning of life and the answer to every emotion. His attraction to women is motivated by his obsession for finding the truth, and often he falls prey to his own intentions by a touch too much promiscuity. The trouble is Scorpios actually need long-term and stable relationships. But the man is dangerous if you are on his hit-list. He'll pursue you secretively at first. If you find you are the chosen one he can also take over your whole existence.

Sometimes Scorpio will adore you until he actually destroys love, and you, in his mind and soul. It's the regenerative process of the Pluto passion, so you might as well enjoy the attention and the ecstasy while you can before he kills the love he has created.

His jealousy is intense. He lives and breathes every emotion, and with it love. He'll surprise you with spicy and secret rendezvous. In bed he'll be the connoisseur of all things sexual and emotional. He will want sex to be a symbolic, esoteric experience that sometimes falls close to obsession. Sex is big business to him and he can justifiably prove it with his reputation of a discreet but highly dangerous lover. But he has incredibly high standards and you must be spotless, almost virginal. The Scorpio male wants all or nothing, and the longer your mystery is prolonged the more intense the turn-on he gets.

You have to be emotionally and mentally strong to have

a relationship with this man. If you think you can handle him, can bear the shock when his eyes start to penetrate another victim's heart across the room, beware! This man is powerful. A boa constrictor takes a very long time to kill its prey – by gently squeezing the life out of it; until it can breathe no more.

THE SCORPIO WOMAN

The powerful seductress of the zodiac takes life seriously, too seriously at times. When she first sets eyes on you she will want to dominate you both physically and emotionally. Scorpio girls have an intuitive awareness of their sexual magnetism and, like sparks of static electricity, you will feel her presence in the room, whether you've met the haunting gaze of her eyes or not.

Watch out when she's about, for this dark, deeply motivated lady can play any charming role, any teasing subtle game that will make you think you are in control, not her.

If she could, the female snake would have been born a man, but as she has to bear the physical weakness of woman, she is more like the Medusa's head than one serpent, and more like a dozen Plutonian meteorites than a simple solitary moon.

For a Water sign she gives a pretty good impression of a Fiery one. Playing the *femme fatale* is easy for she creates subtle intrigue, the mystery and enigmatic power of a genie or a sorcerer. She can be hot and dominating one minute, then an emotional wreck the next. She'll hate voraciously and she'll love passionately. Whatever emotion she feels, she feels with intensity.

If she falls in love with you it will, for that moment, at least be for ever. Playing games with her is fatal, and if you start thinking the relationship should remain casual and lighthearted you might get a shock when she starts calling you on the phone in the middle of the night with tears, threats and demands.

Strength in a man is the Scorpio girl's weakness. The more independent, the more ambitious you are, the more she will love you. Sex and love are like a parasite and its host; without one you can't have the other. Remember, she takes her relationships very seriously and will sacrifice you for another if it means the total fulfilment of her soul.

Power is crucial to her existence and she won't be thwarted. Her strength of character is admirable, and her sexuality is so intense that it could take a lifetime really to know her. Secrets are big words for Scorpio girls, so make sure you have plenty, but keep her own mystery to yourself.

THE SAGITTARIUS MAN

The Archer is born altruistic, bold and voracious. It seems that he has the spirit and the morals of an Angel but watch out, the legendary bowman is more likely to have the soul of a gambler and the morals of a sexual extortionist. With unnerving blind faith and the optimism of Don Quixote this happy-go-lucky man wins his way through life and relationships like a trail of fiery stars. His honest and blunt admission for loving women make him the sort of guy that other men hate and women adore. It's not the egotistic vanity of an Aries, nor the power-driven motivation of a Leo; this Fire sign is genuinely convinced that this is the way things are. He can't help it if he was born beautiful, can he?

He's honest and open about himself, doesn't pretend to be something that he's not, and certainly lets you know if he's had enough of your company. He flirts easily, is really everybody's friend and is lighthearted and easy about life and women.

No strings and no commitments make this man's sense of freedom and need for a blank cheque in personal relationships sacrosanct.

Often the Archer looks for adventure, sexual or otherwise, as long as he can maintain his buccaneering spirit. That is why Sagittarians often resort to casual relationships to make sure there is nothing to stop their capricious wanderings. Meeting challenges head-on is the way the Archer travels through life and love. He responds to the thrill of the chase, of a woman who is hard to pick up. But he is idealistic and if you live up to his high standards he has the uncanny ability to know exactly how things are going to work out with you. If the Archer actually agrees to make an arrangement to meet you the following week and the stars are in his eyes as well as yours, you might think you had instigated the wonderful moment. But Sagittarians have this knack of making you think big, and sharing their expansive nature.

Like the other Fire signs, Sagittarians need outdoor activities and an extrovert lifestyle. If you can keep up with his active and quite fast-paced life he might consider you to be the pal he's looking for. Sex isn't everything to a Sagittarian, he needs someone to play mental and physical games too. He needs an inventive sex life, and his moods can range from passionate and fiery to warm and playful. Sex is fun, not a deep emotional experience.

So don't ever get soppy about him, he really doesn't like the kind of woman who hangs around like a lost doll, or who hasn't a life of her own. The Archer needs someone who is never possessive and rarely jealous, though on occasions he can be.

Watch out for the hailstones though, the Sagittarian can flash in and out of your life like a magnetic storm to avoid those rainclouds of commitment. But if he's convinced you're as free and easy, as unemotional and as unpossessive as he is, then maybe he'll forget about his unreliable and irresponsible attitude to life, and settle for permanent free love. That paradox is what he really wants.

THE SAGITTARIUS WOMAN

The outspoken Archer woman will insist on letting you know if you don't match up to her ideal, and she'll also pull your ideas apart with frank and brutal honesty which, to the uninitiated, can be a cultural shock. She lives independently and is always happier if her freedom isn't curtailed. Her honesty is genuine but it can sometimes cut through your heart like a butter knife, particularly as she's one of the most vivacious, amusing and popular females.

She prefers the company of men in any social setting and openly flirts in a rather innocent and childlike way. Like her Geminian opposite sign, she has no need for emotional depth to her relationships and prefers the surface attractions, the moles and wrinkles of appearances, rather than the viscera of human emotion. Friendship and companionship are more important than close emotional ties, and often platonic relationships with men and keeping friendly with ex-lovers is the easiest way to maintain her freedom and ensure an easy-going existence.

She can be so frank, that discussing her ex-boyfriends' intimate inclinations can sound like boasting to your ear, when she was only just letting you know how absurd she finds the whole sexual game. She doesn't mean to hurt anyone, never means to upset or put down a friend, and will end up confused and embarrassed by her own big mouth.

But an Archer girl's optimism spreads through her life and into her partner's with the ease of ripe brie. To be so confident, to be so sure that a relationship will work as long as she has her freedom, is a bonus to any partnership.

Communicating inner emotions and deeper tensions is not part of her vocabulary and that's why she often confuses love with casual friendship. Sex is also not to be confused with love, and she can have a strong physical relationship with a man and just be good friends. Being a pal is easier, doesn't lead to commitments, to arrangements, and traps like that big word 'love' always seems to do. If she's kept you up all night at a dinner-party, played the life and soul, flirted with your dad, and hardly noticed your jealousy, don't expect her to apologise. Her mind is set, and her morals are high, but she does like to have fun, her own way. If you want her to do anything, always ask nicely, never order her or tell her. She won't be bossed, in public or in private, or in bed.

Don't trap this incurable romantic. Don't question her, and you'll find her free love is all for you!

THE CAPRICORN MAN

The Capricorn male is often likened to that goaty god, Pan. On the surface Pan may be a dour, apparently bloody-minded hard-liner, but somewhere underneath it all you might find some true warmth and a consistently easy-going nature.

Capricorns are often conventional and rarely let themselves slip into any gear other than the one they have selected. In relationships with women they need to be in control. Even a power-mad Pan's chaos is controlled. In the wild abandon of infatuation his feelings and emotions are held from the precipice of freedom. He will be in charge of his destiny and yours, if you so much as show any inkling of desire for him.

He admires women who can coax him out of his stuffy Goat ways. But he also likes women who are ambitious for him too. Can this bedrock of society really rock the sexual and emotional bed? If he never deviates from his own tethering circle, will he ever have fun? A few women can release him from his rope of cold love. His inner nature often mellows as he ages, and oddly enough the paradox of this man is that as he gets older and more conventional he will also let go of any sexual inhibitions and allow spontaneous 'feelings' to enter his heart.

Pan often gets involved with women just for financial or

career advancement. You'll often meet rich and successful females who have been taken advantage of by a Goat. Some of them have the man tethered on the dry arid plain of a monotonous marriage, but most of these Goats are already up there at the top of the mountain. The funny thing is that a Capricorn can digest all the flack you might throw at him for using you. A Goat's stomach speaks for itself!

The Capricorn man is shatterproof and biodegradable. Once he's decided you're the partner for his tenacious way of life, then he'll want to run you as smoothly as his business.

He can seem cold and passionless, restrained and indelicate in sexual communication. He is awfully possessive and it's very hard to change his opinions. But the taciturn Goat has a dry and witty sense of humour and there's always that twinge of inner warmth to draw out. He's not dull, but his approach to sex can be as disciplined and as ambitious as his approach to work. There is a closet romantic in his heart trying desperately to get out, and he needs a wise woman to open the door for him. As long as your relationship is within the boundaries of his own white lines, and he is in control, you'll find the most loyal and reliable partner behind those wardrobe doors.

THE CAPRICORN WOMAN

Don't ever expect a romantic encounter with this woman to last very long. She'll have all those graceful, feminine wiles, make all those suggestive noises about a full-scale affair, but the kissing and the innuendos and the candlelit dinners will last only as long as she wants them to. And that is often shorter than you'd imagined!

The Goat lady is always ambitious and she knows what she wants. If she wants you, she'll look beyond the romantic aspect of love for something more stable, more gutsy and more to do with a business arrangement than an emotional one.

She is often power-mad, whether it's in the office, or in a relationship. There's no point floundering around in bed making wild romantic promises, and sharing ideals when you can go for the real thing. A commitment, a permanent relationship. She doesn't relax in love easily and has a cool approach to sex and emotions. But if you give this Goat the lead she can be intensely passionate and will gradually lose her shyness once she's known you a long time. She has to control the affair her own way, but don't let her fool you into thinking her calm and bossy approach is the only backbone to her heart and her head. Her feathers are easily ruffled and, although she doesn't live in the twilight zone of feelings, she can get jealous and brood quite easily, and sulk if she feels slighted or betrayed.

She needs to know exactly where she's going in life and with you. Self-imposed discipline makes her sometimes pessimistic and will convince her that love is as shallow as your first kiss in the back of the black cab. Capricorn girls find intimate relationships difficult to handle unless they are really in charge, and that's why they make excellent partners or wives, but not very wonderful lovers.

The Goat lady needs her home and her mountain to climb. If she is sure you are worth pursuing she'll also ensure that she is ambitious for you too. A lot of Capricorn ladies are the true reason behind a man's career success! If you can let her take the lead through the chaos of emotion, not burden her with demanding encounters and weak-willed indecision, then she'll stay at the top of the one mountain she yearns to climb with you, called love.

THE AQUARIUS MAN

You have to remember that the space-age man is an unconventional and eccentric freedom lover, and yet wants to be everyone's friend and stick to his own quite rigid lifestyle. Aquarian men set out to find as many friends as they possibly can, rather than worry about love and sex. Love and sex are valid, and part of life, but they aren't the be-all of existence for this fixed Air sign. As long as the Water-Bearer sees change and progress in others, or in the world around him, then he is blissfully happy. He does not particularly pursue or encourage it in himself.

Our Uranus man is an out-of-space man. He's an oddball, a weirdo, often the man you meet at the office disco who doesn't drink and doesn't dance but smokes a pipe and looks like an anarchist. He might also be that man on the commuter train you see every morning who gazes at you with alien eyes and has an aloof and rather cold appearance. He's actually silently working you out, because Aquarians, like Frankenstein, enjoy scientific investigation of the human psyche!

His feelings about women can be as cranky as his habits, but there is one thing he will always do first before he makes any move to attempt a relationship: convince himself that you are strong enough to cope with his inquisitive and probing mind.

He feels it's his right to know everything about the woman of his choice, and the deeper the mystery you stir, the longer you remain an enigma, the more likely he'll want to nose-dive into your secrets. So make sure your game of 'catch me when you can' involves a worthwhile solution!

The secret of the universe, your sexual appetite, you name it, the Aquarian will unravel the truth to expose the answers. Sex is no less, no more, important than any other facet of his active life, and if you're happy to consider sex and love as part of your life too, then you'll stand a better chance of a long-term relationship with this man and all his friends.

Love is impersonal to an Aquarian. He takes it and hands it round with the same degree of feeling (and that's an awfully hard word for him to say) to everyone. Don't ever think that you are special. You can be part of his life, but never to the exclusion of others. Being friends is more important than being lovers. This is how he will choose a soul-mate: sex comes second to this Air sign who lives in his head and rarely in his heart.

He enjoys sex but as for other Air signs it's fun, a mental experience, not emotional, and definitely not soppy. Aquarius is an abstract lover who will blow cold rather than hot. He'll persist until he strips the outer bark of your personality like an icy wind bares the most beautiful and toughest trees. If you're still in one piece and agree to be his pal, that is what counts. Who needs lovers, when you can have a good and permanent friend?

THE AQUARIUS WOMAN

Possessions and possessiveness are not something an Aquarian woman will even consider in her emotional or sexual relationships, particularly from her partner. Her unpredictable and unconventional approach to life is formulated from a stubborn need to be awkward for the sake of it.

She needs mental rapport, companionship, and above all, friendship with a man: someone she can talk to all night and all day, who will stand by her, be loyal and genuine and caring about humanity as well as about the individual long before she'll even consider him as a possible mate in bed or in the home. Aquarian women often live alone better than with apartner and spend a good deal of their lives independently succeeding in careers rather than in motherhood.

The Uranian girl's emotional detachment keeps her free from forming too intense and personal relationships. It gives her an open lifestyle, the chance to encounter as many friends as she possibly can. If you can be her friend and not attempt to own her or try to change her and accept that you have to share her with the world as she shares you with the world, then you may have found a soul-mate. Her apparent lack of passion can be frustrating, but her loyalty is impeccable and her stability is supportive.

Passion implies commitment and intensity, and to an Aquarian girl both are abhorrent. She enjoys sex and physical contact as a pleasurable and warm activity between friends, but she won't ever let you get soppy or slushy. If you do she'll think you're weak and pathetic, and she needs a tower of strength in her bed, not a fragile sandcastle. She can take sex, or leave it.

The essence of an Aquarian girl's love is based on her need to force herself to be different, to be an eccentric. She will, of course, have delved into your mind, wriggled out your intentions, and scanned you with an emotional barium meal to check out if you're worthy of closer inspection. But if friendship isn't in your heart, then love and sex won't be in hers.

THE PISCES MAN

If you've ever gone fishing out at sea, on the glimmering darkling patches of the ocean where the water is black and the bottom of the sea runs deeper than the height of the tallest mountain, then you'll know exactly what a Pisces man is like to catch. Often you have to climb into that diving bell, and take a powerful torch to locate him. Sometimes he'll emerge only to escape from life into fiction and fantasy. He'll often prefer to drown in anything, as long as it's drowning.

Fish men are charmingly romantic and awfully attractive

because they are such dreamers; a very different challenge from the passion of Fire signs, the mental agility and lightness of Air or the solid practicality and sensuality of Earth men.

Impressionable to the point of being blotting pads, they will see only what they want to see and cloud their incredible intuitive and psychic senses with careless indecision. Mr Denizen-of-the-Deep lives in a partial eclipse of life no matter what love-encounters throw at him. He is easily led astray by alcohol and women. The Fish will escape into shadowland and pretty dreams, rather than face the mundane reality of life. If he fails in a relationship it's simple: he retreats. For someone who is actually quite gregarious he drifts through life as the zodiacal mop, absorbing and sensing your changing moods.

The Fish men are drawn to very beautiful and very female women. They are easily besotted by physical beauty. Being in love is a good escape from real life, whether it's with a beautiful day, a beautiful drink, or beautiful women. You can lead a Piscean astray more easily than you can get a dog to eat a bag of crisps, and you can get him into an intimate sexual relationship faster than a black-cab meter spends your money.

Sexually he is uniquely gifted. He doesn't need words or books, passion and emotion flow easily and love grows quickly in his deep cave of feelings. But Piscean men are often too far away in their own fantasy, and if you're not open with him you'll get left behind on the shore while he's diving back down into the deepest part of the ocean for the water spirits.

This half-man, half-fish is only ever half-seen. If you are prepared to embark on a sea voyage with him, make sure you've got the sea-legs to follow him to the deepest part of the ocean when he leaves you for his own lonely ecstasy.

THE PISCES WOMAN

The mermaid is half-fish, half-girl, and the Pisces girl is half-way between reality and a dreamworld, far from any logical or mental plane, in a world of intuition and feelings. She is usually poised, beautiful, and compassionate. Love and caring is genuinely felt, and she is kind and uniquely sensitive to others around her. She is the girl who sells sea-shells on the sea-shore, a poetry of emotional fluidity.

Of course this kind of feminine mystique attracts men easily, so she is usually surrounded by a choice of the best fish in the sea. There are many Piscean women who have been badly hurt by rushing headlong into romantic involvements without a thought because they really do not think. The Mermaid suffers intensely from emotional pain, and bitterness can turn her fishy scales to higher melancholy octaves. She can be led astray by the temptation of romance, or by the masks of drugs or alcohol to hide from her own passionate feelings. The Mermaid is deep to find. Like diving for oyster pearls, she will be hidden, unfathomable, and never in shallow water. Her elusive nature is vague and sometimes dithery, and she will always be moving somewhere and never be sure where it is she should be going.

Love is a touch-down, a grounding from reality and she'll fall into it as easily as Alice fell down the rabbit hole. In love she gets carried away by emotion and the prevailing moods of her lover can channel her through the murkiest waters and the shimmering waves like driftwood. Yet sometimes the physical intensity of her sexuality will produce emotional conflicts within herself and she will begin to see the man she thought she loved as just another shell on her lovely sea-shore. She is like the tide that washes across the empty bay, surfing back the shells to find the one that glistens in the sun, rather than the ones that turn to sand. She needs to belong to the sea of love, and to one man, and that man must be strong and protective, and mostly understanding.

The Mermaid often falls for weak, nebulous and gifted characters, a lover who makes love and feels as deeply as she. But together they will drown each other. The tide that carries her on to a better shore is the man who turns up the oyster bed and finds the real pearls inside.

The 12 Signs as Friends

ARIES

The Aries friend is rather like a meteorite landing in your life. Full of energy and enthusiasm for your friendship one day, the next deserting you for another planet, leaving you feeling deserted. Ariens can make and break friendships faster than any other sign. They hate being dependent on anyone and, on the whole, would rather have many acquaintances than close pals. Ariens of both sexes enjoy the companionship of men, and the rough and tumble of fairly lively and noisy gatherings, but they can be quite happy with their own company. They find it difficult to keep platonic relationships with the other sex and are not known for their reliability as friends. They would rather ensure they are the centre of attention so, if others are prepared to tag along with them, they may just be pally while the going is good!

TAURUS

Bulls of both sexes make warm and considerate friends. They need close, intimate friends rather than loose and casual ones and prefer the company of individual pals to social gatherings. They are always generous and would prefer you borrow from them, rather than owe you any favour, yet they are genuinely concerned for your welfare. They need a lot of affection and tactile communication, bear-hugs and cheek-kissing, rather than just a nod, both from friends of their own sex and platonic friends of the other. They like to feel comfortable and will make great efforts to make you always feel at home in their own nests. If you ever need to phone for help, a Taurean is just the sort of person to get you out of trouble, without getting het up, but they may take their time getting there!

GEMINI

Gemini loves a varied and lively social life. Not very reliable when you make arrangements for outings, they are not very fond of very intimate, close friendships. They prefer a wide circle of acquaintances to the serious one-to-one friend. However, they are so adaptable that they will make friends very quickly, chatter about the world and generally enjoy themselves. They can be inconsistent, and also gossips in big circles, so as a close and trusted friend they are not really reliable. Both sexes like platonic friendships, and you often find they have more true friends of the opposite sex than they do of their own. Very gregarious, but not very loyal, they also like to feel they can leave when they want to, rather than have any restrictions to adhere to. They need friends who enjoy intellectual pursuits rather than the great outdoors. But they are adaptable, and will try anything new, for the sake of novelty.

CANCER

Crabs take a long time to make friends and therefore prefer to make firm relationships with people they can trust and have known for a long time. They don't enjoy big gatherings, and rooms full of people they don't know, but will enjoy socialising if it's among small groups of similar-minded people. Can be surprisingly obsessive about maintaining a close friendship and need to feel they can rely on someone to talk through all their own fears and woes. Cancerians are generally cautious about lending money, or any of their possessions, and don't particularly like being asked about their finances. Although they insist on depending on their close friends, they are also easily hurt if let down by others and can take it very much to heart. But they are wonderful at helping in a crisis, and will never let you down.

LEO

The Lion likes to roar and be the centre of attention in any social gathering. They make friends easily with both sexes and will often have a very wide circle of friends to amuse their ego-orientated heads. Leos make good friends and are more reliable than the other Fire signs. They are intensely loyal and will stick up for any one of their acquaintances if they get into trouble, or need supporting. Though not emotionally close to new friends, nor even to the old and trusted, they do need warmth and a fun-loving rapport to stay your pal for long. They are open-hearted and quite generous, but don't ever betray their trust or they can scratch back. Most Leos love socialising and parties, and are often the all-night party goers rather than the dinner party type.

VIRGO

They make difficult friends as they never quite get close enough to anyone, nor accept other people for what they are. They can be cold and judgmental, and also, once they think they know you, can seem quite critical. Yet they are good at socialising on a wider scale, and enjoy casual acquaintances and brief friendships so that they don't get caught up in emotion. On a wider scale they will be lively, fun to be with and enjoy intellectual and stimulating company. They are very cautious about who they invite into their house, and often prefer not to venture into other people's homes: it gets too warm! They like general chit-chat and would prefer to chat to friends in the pub and not make any commitments nor rely on others for anything. They are very single-minded but can be relied upon to organise any event or social gathering. Societies and clubs are their favourite way of keeping acquaintances around them and not getting tied down.

LIBRA

Libra is the most sociable and affable of signs. Librans love parties, social gatherings of all kinds and will always want to make friends with as many people as they possibly can. Librans are also quite a dab hand at keeping in touch with old friends, and they look on casual acquaintances with as much sympathy as they do someone they've known since childhood. Librans need a lot of company and don't enjoy the solitary life. As close friends they can be relied on, but they often have a habit of appearing interested in what you have to say when in fact their mind is somewhere else. They are not particularly deep, nor passionate about forming a close bond unless a friend is prepared to make an effort too. They love gossip and small talk, and don't enjoy lengthy philosophical discussions

SCORPIO

Scorpios are slow to make friends but, when they do, they make them for life. They aren't too fond of large gatherings, but may appear on the surface quite charming and outgoing. Underneath they are probably testing you out to see if you live up to their incredibly high standards! Most Scorpios need very close and intense friendships. Because it takes them so long to decide whether they have found a true and confidential pal, they often find that they lose friends quickly. They don't like to rely on anyone, but they will provide all the emotional support that anyone could need, and have admirable shoulders to cry on. Scorpios can usually and intuitively know if someone is a fair-weather friend but, once a bond is formed, they want it to be unbreakable and don't respond well to casual, light and inconsistent friendships.

SAGITTARIUS

Archers usually have a wide circle of friends, and prefer light and easy pals to any deep and meaningful ones! They move around so much that they are likely to make friends with strangers in the street. They are never suspicious, and never cautious and, if a friend turns out to be an enemy, they can shrug their shoulders and bear no malice, as they just move on to another one. Their open and freedom-loving approach to life makes them fairly unreliable friends to have. Although they can enjoy the company of their own sex and play light amusing games, they aren't good at any form of permanence. They don't like making arrangements and would prefer just to turn up when they feel like it. Both sexes like platonic relationships and feel more comfortable surrounded by many rather than a few.

CAPRICORN

Rather stuck in their ways, Capricorns are not good at making friends and not easy to make friends with! Both sexes prefer the company of men, and would rather form any relationship on a business arrangement than anything looser. They don't need a wide or varied social life and enjoy the company of a few friends who share the same ambitions or mental stimulation. Once they do form any strong friendship, they will try to keep it for life and do not take kindly to being let down. They are not particularly interested in giving or going to parties, and would rather talk in the boardroom or the pub where they feel safer in a neutral environment.

AQUARIUS

Aquarians are naturals at making friends; and keeping them. They love to have a wide variety and circle of friends, and will insist on maintaining endless platonic relationships to ensure that their altruism is genuinely felt. They are in need of mental rapport rather than any sporting or clubby basis for friendship. They are consistent and determined to supply any mental or emotional support they can handle. Although rather cold emotionally, they will always analyse friends' problems and crack the truth, rather than lead you into false promises. Although they prefer people with cranky or eccentric minds like their own, Aquarians enjoy the company of anyone who can stimulate them intellectually. They always say what they mean, and can often be awkward about your judgments. But they will never let you down in a crisis

PISCES

Pisceans are only slow to make friends as they are a little wary, for all their gregarious nature. They mix well in neutral surroundings and enjoy informal parties and gatherings where they can merge in with the crowd. They enjoy friends of both sexes and prefer to feel relaxed and non-committal rather than have pressures and obligations forced on them. They make wonderful friends when a rapport is established and are genuinely sympathetic, genuinely compassionate and always ready to help with any emotional comfort or support. They prefer a strong mental and intuitive friendship but can be too impressionable and soak up others' problems and bad habits rather than remaining independent of them. They often have a large circle of acquaintances and don't often have many close friends. Pisceans usually have one very old friend to rely on in times of trouble.

Some Famous Aquarians

Christian Dior (21 January 1905)
John Hurt (22 January 1940)
HSH Princess Caroline of Monaco (23 January 1957)
Jeanne Moreau (Z3 January 1928)
Natassya Kinski (24 January 1961)
Virginia Woolf (25 January 1882)
Michael Bentine (26 January 1922)
Lewis Carroll (27 January 1832)
Wolfgang Amadeus Mozart (27 January 1756)
Mikhail Baryshnikov (28 January 1948)
Phil Collins (30 January 1951)
Vanessa Redgrave (30 January 1937)
Tallulah Bankhead (31 January 1903)
Nell Gwynn (2 February 1650)
Charlotte Rampling (5 February 1946)
Patrick MacNee (6 February 1922)
Peter Jay (7 February 1937)
Charles Dickens (7 February 1812)
James Dean (8 February 1931)
Joyce Grenfell (10 February 1910)
Burt Reynolds (11 February 1936)
Abraham Lincoln (12 February 1809)
Oliver Reed (13 February 1938)
Claire Bloom (15 February 1931)
Patricia Routledge (17 February 1929)

AQUARIUS COUPLES

Business partners, past and present

David Jason (2 February 1940) and
Nicholas Lyndhurst (Aries – 20 April 1961)
Jack Lemmon (8 February 1925) and
Walter Matthau (Libra – I October 1920)
Don Everly (1 February 1937) and
Phil Everly (Capricorn – 19 January 1939)
Frank Muir (5 February 1920) and
Denis Norden (Aquarius – 6 February 1922)

Romantic couples, past and present

Paul Newman (26 January 1925) and
Joanne Woodward (Pisces – 27 February 1930)
Libby Purves (2 February 1950) and
Paul Heiney (Aries – 20 April 1949)
Mia Farrow (9 February 1945) and
Woody Allen (Sagittarius – 1 December 1935)
John McEnroe (16 February 1959) and
Tatum O'Neal (Scorpio – 5 Novem~er 1963)
Yoko Ono Lennon (18 February 1934) and
John Lennon (Libra 9 October 1940)
Eva Braun (6 February 1912) and
Adolph Hitler (Taurus – 20 April 1889)
Sinead Cusack (18 February 1948) and
Jeremy Irons (Virgo – 19 September 1948)

Astro Meditations

**FOR YOU AND YOUR PARTNER
FOR 1994–1995.**

ARIES

Being first in everything is being part of everything. Use your energy and impulse creatively, spontaneously. Be you, but learn from gentleness. Fire is cosmic, don't burn others up, set them alight instead.

TAURUS

Hedonistic, jewels of sensuality. Pursue pleasures instead of waiting for them. Resentment builds on regrets. Take notice of energy, ground it if you must. Endurance is an art – respect it.

GEMINI

Seek change, but seek change within. Don't try to look deeper, you can't. The surface is coloured, is covered in shimmering. Let it be superficial, let your sexual love and lightness glide.

CANCER

Be a lunatic but face the truth that you have deeper emotions. Insecurity is instability. Sex and love can unite. Don't hide yourself from your truth – you are an introvert/extrovert. Light a candle to yourself.

LEO

Self-gratification. You love to impress, to make a noise, to have power. Power can be constructive, love and sexuality instructive. Flash warmth. Roar with pride rather than conceit.

VIRGO

Let go of the sex manual. Take a trip on surprise, on unpredictability, that is love. Stop worrying – be dippy. Perfect diffidence, it is as refreshing as your crisp mentality. Jog in bed, dissent.

LIBRA

Romance is born easily. Use charm explosively, no time for hesitation. Fall in love with love, but make it clear to yourself. Clarify romantic attraction and know it for what it is.

SCORPIO

Sentence only your obsessions. Keep others' mysteries as proof of emotions. You feel love as sexuality, as wholeness – the mystery and the answer to life. Fulfil your needs tenderly, administer with light.

SAGITTARIUS

You can expand, let others know. Give yourself freely, without blunt words. Wise to the world, wise eventually in love. Try loyalty, let go of promiscuity. Challenge sexual egotism with altruistic love.

CAPRICORN

Treat sex as an infant, nurture it. Grow with it, not against it. Try reaching out, try giving with the heart. There is no power in restriction, in restraint. Tie sex to love instead of to the bed.

AQUARIUS

Rebellion hurts others. Convention can work. Friendship is your heaven – let others come closer, let others conform if they must. Sex can be part of love, not a trap, it can be free.

PISCES

Ideals, half-seen, half-being. The stray are led astray more easily than the homed. The clouds can open with rainbows on the ocean. Take a deep-sea dive, communicate love instead of drowning.

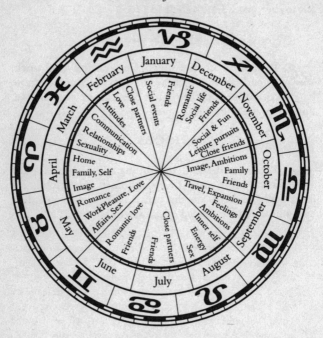

*Your at-a-glance chart showing
love trends for 1995*

Aquarius

The inner sections emphasise the important moods and
trends through each month of 1995 with regard to love,
friendship, partnership, sex.

Aquarius

COMPATIBILITIES

AQUARIUS MAN – AQUARIUS WOMAN

The individualistic spirit of two Aquarians together is often, to an outsider, an extremist relationship where both seem to lead separate lives and really have little to do with one another. Actually this is far from the truth. When they first meet, the Aquarians' natural inclination is to be platonic and close friends. There may be a hint of sexual desire, a knowing that they are so similar and that sex will probably be good between them. But that is not why they become involved, and it is the last reason why they actually stay in a permanent partnership.

They are both fascinated by life and the theories that they can make about it. The Aquarian girl may be less inventive, but she is just as cranky in her habits and often much pushier and more stubborn than the Aquarian male. They both think love is about friendship, and any romantic involvement always comes later rather than sooner. Essentially they are mistrustful and often cynical about romantic and sexual love. Both are so single-minded that they will often have their own exclusive circle of friends. Abstract Air signs are able to understand each other's need to live an extra-terrestrial form of life. They may be mentally in tune, and reasonable about each other's freedom, but what they often find troublesome is the unfortunate fact that both are extremely stubborn about their own weird habits. This can produce tension when she wants to eat breakfast at the kitchen able, and he insists on having his in the garden. The Aquarian girl will never be able to persuade him otherwise, and she is certainly not going to change her ways to suit anyone. They like trying to change others and, if they meet with resistance, they can turn very cold, which is why their relationship can often appear indifferent. But if they have established a firm friendship, and this they trust deeply because they both will have analysed it to the core before they even decided to become hitched, they are generally fixed enough to stick together like a pair of outlaws.

AQUARIUS MAN – PISCES WOMAN

The Fish out of water can sense the ideals of the Aquarian man before she realises that his detached attitude to life will always make him aloof and rather cold. A Pisces woman needs his type of strength and determination, but she can do without the analysis and the constant reminder that he is not interested in individual, only humanitarian love. She will agree. In fact the Fish people are also very much concerned with compassion and the welfare of others, over and above themselves and their true strength lies in their ability to rise like dolphins in moments of crisis. Pisces women, sensitive and sometimes gullible as they seem, are fighters for their ideals as much as their partners, and the Aquarian man could find that a Fish is better equipped at handling his detached and Airy dissidence better than most. She will have to learn to tolerate his temperamental attitude to problems, for he must always solve them, however insignificant they appear to anyone else. He's the first to investigate the reason why there are dog turds in their garden. She won't particularly care why and would be happier just shovelling them in the earth. But the know-it-all Aquarian will be down there with his magnifying glass, and possibly a few plastic bags, to perform an autopsy and check out which dog it was. Colour, breed, sex, you name it, the Aquarian will find out the answer.

The Aquarian's ability to play the forensic scientist is an irritation from which the Fish girl will wish to escape. Sexually he can't really give her the affection and indulgence she needs, and she is too ephemeral and emotional for his own peculiar taste. It's not that she doesn't agree with his high ideals, nor that she loves change and non-conformity any less than he, but she really can't be bothered with inspection and analysis. Retreating is easier, and the Aquarian must accept that she may well disappear quite frequently for solitude or for being with her own circle of less ineffectual friends.

AQUARIUS WOMAN – PISCES MAN

The benevolent and quite sincerely compassionate Piscean man can find a lot in common with the independent and highly spirited Aquarian girl. For starters, they are both idealistic. He lives in dreams and she is attracted by the intangibilities of life. Theorising her problems, her ideas and her thoughts can become addictive with this very receptive and intuitive man. She will find that life never gets boring with him, because he is constantly shifting ideas, changing his attitudes and generally slipping around the ocean like a poetic flying Fish. They need their individual freedom. She will often have a very separate life from his and he often disappears into dream land to escape from reality. She will mind if he doesn't tell her (she does like to be informed about everything), but she realises that her own freedom is important too and will learn to respect his quieter one.

The mental affinity between them is what counts first. The Aquarian girl will probably have made friends with this man a long time before she actually embarks on a more romantic or sexual relationship with him. But Fish make friends easily, and he'll be easy-going about his emotions, letting them stay hidden in the darker caves of his mind and heart until he feels she is ready to accept them. He is not a particularly decisive person, but he is able to switch off from the truth if need be. He will not happily face conflict or emotional scenes. Aquarians aren't emotional types either, but they do flare up and get on their high horses if things aren't done how they think they should be done. Her stubbornness could be the reason the Fish gets uptight, and the Fish hates having his sea disturbed! He will quite rightly put his own case forward, however visionary and idealistic it is, and often, because the Aquarian feeds on such unconventional behaviour, she will begin to enjoy the Fish's more inconsistent and inconstant nature, by the very fact that he is such a non-conformist himself. Living with her awkward strain to be different won't be easy for a Fish, he needs peace and solitude, but he also needs someone just a bit crazy like himself.

AQUARIUS MAN – ARIES WOMAN

Aries women are number one in their own life, and also number one in every relationship. If she doesn't win the risks and the dice rolls of love that she's set her heart on, then she can storm out of a man's life quicker than she stormed into it. With an Aquarian man she is never quite sure if she is winning. He is capable of an almost devious game in which he will never let on who he is or what he really wants. This can infuriate the Aries girl, but only makes him a more challenging prospect. His friendship is important, his social life revolves with apparent unselfishness, and yet he is always holding something back. She can never be sure if it's love he feels or humanitarian compassion. The Aries girl wants to be the be-all of his life, but the Aquarian is more generous with his love and would rather share himself and his relationship with the world. This can make an Aries woman invariably jealous, and it can cause a strain whereby she never feels superior, and he really doesn't have the time to begin to care.

Sexually she will enjoy running the show to begin with but an Aquarian doesn't like being bossed around, as much as he doesn't want to be the boss. Eventually their bedtime fun will suffer when his aloof and sometimes cold passion deflates her vulnerable but beautiful ego.

AQUARIUS WOMAN – ARIES MAN

A brilliant but probably short-lived affair. The Aquarian girl will probably check out everything about this man before even allowing him near her front door, let alone her bed. He will be after a far more physical relationship than she is. But if the Aries man can accept friendship as the most important part of their relationship, they may stand a good chance. Aries men want adventure and excitement in bed, romance and the promise of passionate fulfilment. The Aquarian girl is more likely to be interested in his brain and he may not be quirky enough to amuse her for long. But Aquarian women must defy convention and maybe the sexual antics of this egotistic man will keep her fascinated longer than she imagined. Like most Air signs, her boredom level is reached more quickly than anyone else's and, if he can keep her mind active as well as her body, they will need little emotion in their relationship. Sexual activity is only part of the whole deal to an Aquarian, but to an Aries it represents his ego. She might want intimate conversation by the Thames at midnight, and an awful lot of respect. He might just want a night making love in a tent on a bare mountain. She is an anarchist, and sometimes Aries can be incredibly old-fashioned. This is where they differ deeply. Intellectually Aries men aren't quite on the same planet; it's almost as if they've been left on Mars when the Aquarian girl took off for Earth, and a better place. She might encourage him to think laterally, but her individual and odd habits will leave him cold.

AQUARIUS MAN – TAURUS WOMAN

The aloof and unresponsive Aquarian man has great trouble dealing with the warm responsive Taurean woman who has just touched his arm and offered to cook him dinner at his place one night. The distance this man puts between himself and a possible romantic involvement is further than Uranus from Earth, and this is where these two are far apart. He is Uranus, and she is the Earth: erotic, tactile, needing all the sensual and romantic notions to sharpen her determined and committed motives. Uranians can only be the awkward, straining, unconventional friend who really would rather study your books and work out your background than fall into bed and into love.

Earthy Taurus will want to put her hand round his as soon as she feels comfortable in his presence. But the trouble with Aquarians is that they really have no need for any physical contact. They live resolutely in their heads and no one is going to change their dippy behaviour, especially not such a warm and trusting woman as a Bull. Some Aquarians have been known to get quickly allergic to a girl's cat, just to avoid getting into a relationship. He needs to live alone with a million friends, and a million ideas to test. He wants considerable freedom in a relationship, and a lonely Aquarian is better than a restricted one. Permanency with a possessive woman will cramp his unpredictable and eccentric behaviour. He can find peace with a like-minded being, but the Taurean is too different, too real, and too much of a woman for him. If he falls in love with her it will be short-lived and relies on the fact only that she can tolerate his madness!

AQUARIUS WOMAN – TAURUS MAN

Aquarians are eccentric and radical, both intellectually and sexually. Taurus is conservative and basic in his own love life. The Airy woman isn't usually turned on by erotic and sensual sex, she also needs mental fantasy or intellectual excitement to appreciate the truth of tactile feeling. Aquarians are abstract lovers, and Taureans are direct, forthright and feel the sensual pleasures in life. The Aquarian woman will admire his straightforward motives but, unless she is also in one of her equally direct moods, she can turn him off more quickly than her personal convictions can. This can spill over into their bedtime routine like HP sauce. The Aquarian girl shares with the Taurean the ability to choose stubbornness for its own sake, and why should she clean up their domestic rows, when he makes no effort either? Pig-headed people get on well on the surface, but once they become pig-headed with each other there's a volatile relationship on the cards.

Taurus will seem incredibly selfish about sex to the rather colder and independent-minded Aquarian who is more interested in the invention of the wheel than the local cookery classes and washing the dishes. She won't be told when to go to bed any more than she will be told when to get up. The Bull won't be able to cope with her non-conformist sallies down the local pub either. She may be tempted to put him down publicly, her abstraction of his character may seem a simple test to her, but, for a Bull, it will not only outrage his dignity but also his manhood. He has to feel the dominant partner, and it could be very hard with this self-assured woman. Not a very good match as they are both too self-opinionated, and the Bull's pride is easily deflated by the Aquarian girl's lack of warmth or any genuine sexual response.

AQUARIUS MAN – GEMINI WOMAN

Both Air signs, but she is mutable, restless and changing; he is fixed and stubborn, wanting the world to change rather than him. Luckily for the Aquarian man, the Gemini woman rather likes flitting from job to job, or desire to desire. But unluckily for the Gemini girl, the Aquarian man, although mentally in tune with her, can seem dull and too regularly stuck in the mud. At first she will be amused by his strange advances: not like most men who instantly attempt to guide her towards the bedroom, but more like Frankenstein, who would love to create a monster out of her mind! The Aquarian actually finds her impossibly devious, and has a hard time picking her brain and, of course, the further he has to delve, the more likely he is to be sure that she will prove an intellectual equal and perhaps even be worth considering for a permanent relationship. Neither of them desires commitment. The Aquarian has a need for a rather oblique loneliness and independence. He has to have friends, or he'll die but, within that circle, however close, he will remain aloof and free-spirited. Tying herself to an Aquarian may be the funniest thing she's ever done. She will adore his sudden and weird behaviour, and he will get turned on by her spontaneous and Airy lightness about life, including him. She will at times take him too lightly, maybe frustrated by his commitment to emancipation but, ironically, this can often keep her sparked and interested. For her restless nature feeds on dissension as long as it is not of her own making.

Sexually they are fairly similar: emotion and sensuality aren't for them particularly necessary in bed. In fact they would both prefer to talk all night about the universe, set their deckchairs up on the lawn at midnight and watch the stars.

AQUARIUS WOMAN – GEMINI MAN

The nosy Gemini man will find a great deal of genuine, though not emotional sympathy from the equally inquisitive Aquarian girl. She will immediately want to dissect the bright, witty man she's found at the party, and he will at once be talking non-stop about everything, teasing her with words, playing a game of his own while at the same time checking out what she is all about. They both have the same easy attitude to life, although at times the Aquarian can be downright stubborn and downright awkward, if she chooses. Being awkward is not a Geminian trait. He will always want to express himself, and getting out of tricky situations is as much fun to him as getting into them. Getting into a nosegay of Aquarian eccentricity is better than good; not only will her unpredictability keep him on his toes, but her mentality can champion his own. But the Uranian girl will at times find the mood changes of this youthful rogue just as capricious as her own change in stance. She needs a friend first and a lover second. For a Gemini this is the perfect balance for his wide variety of free-range ideas. He has emotions that change with the wind and she has emotions that remain constant but cold. Together they can unlock each other from the fear of failure which they both possess about their sexuality.

AQUARIUS MAN – CANCER WOMAN

The more a Crab girl attempts to circumnavigate this cranky man with her ideals about home life, permanence and stability, about emotional input and sexual fulfilment, the more the Aquarian will run for his independence and resort to his full and varied circle of friends. If he met her, was fascinated by her ability to keep every secret back from him, he will be determined (for Aquarians are awfully stubborn) to find out everything he can before he can attempt to analyse forming a relationship with her. His rather aloof glamour will have attracted her initially; she can appear very aloof too. She loves his sense of fun and his rather strange behaviour which is always fighting against tradition. This is where his fixed attitude lies: not to change and rebel inwardly against the normal constraints of society, but to see society and those around him change with the world. He has the catharsis of others at heart, not his own. The Cancerian girl is very adaptable, she has to be because of that shifting Moon, but she is not fond of change. If the

Aquarian man digs deep enough and finds her emotional responses too intense, he may expect her to give up her secrets and be as crazy about living as he. She is serious about everything; he is serious but only about his effect on abstraction. The Moon girl needs to take a position of control in their relationship, and he will certainly find this unacceptable. He not only needs freedom and a lot of choice in his friendships, but also he certainly won't be tied down to commitment.

Sex is something he's always enjoyed, as any other pleasure. He can over-analyse, and is not exactly filled with deep feelings, but he can provide the passion, for she instils in him a need to find out exactly what is going on in her heart, and in her head. Her secretiveness is her magnetism for this man, and he won't rest until he finds out what all this love and tenderness is about.

AQUARIUS WOMAN – CANCER MAN

The lunatic in the corner will not obviously show his intentions towards any girl. He is a flippant impressionist at times and, at others, the cynical blues player. These extremes of behaviour remind the Aquarian woman that she might like to quiz this man about his inner nature when she begins to suss him out, and she will become more fascinated by his antics when he poses no threat to her quirkiness. Aquarians believe everyone should be their friends, and the constant struggle to keep all their present and past relationships going is part of their stubborn need to be different. The Aquarian woman is nosy, not with the inquisitive curiosity of a Gemini, because she wants to bare the facts, the sordid details of life and then, if a man lives up to her analysis, he might find a place in her social calendar. Unpredictable as ever, she is most likely to instigate a meeting with a Crab. The independent spirit and genuine friendliness of this girl will make the Crab feel comfortable and at home (which is where he likes to be immediately).

He may step out of that shell just for a while and agree to ridiculous and alien behaviour. To the Crab any behaviour which is unconventional has got to be attractive. He is often the most conventional and passive of signs when it comes to love, and this girl isn't. Sooner or later the Crab will begin to resent her blunt speech, and her inquiring mind. He has secrets that he desperately wants to admit to, even to himself. To be strung up like an intellectual and emotional corpse will make him retreat fast. Cancerians really like their love and their partner's love to be exclusive and Aquarians don't. The other problem is that Aquarian women aren't too bothered about sex. They like it, of course, but it has nothing to do with love. Love is between friends, good friends; being in love is about romance, and sex, – well, sex is somewhere in the middle. It's fun, and fun with a Crab is a matter of luck and the Moon. Of course, she might laugh at his conventional ideas, put him into a black mood of rejection and the termination of their relationship will seem inevitable. It usually is, unless they can appreciate each other's very different qualities.

AQUARIUS MAN – LEO WOMAN

The Aquarian man will immediately want to unravel the secrets of the Leo woman's character. She is so full of up-front insolence and so full of passion he can hardly believe why he is so attracted to her. The Lion lady will not be particularly surprised by his aloof interest in her. Most men are interested in Leo ladies, and she really can pick and choose most of the time. But this rather Bohemian man, resembling a mad scientist or an anarchist, is not so much fascinated by her image and her shining, regal appearance but by something actually inside her. He will analyse her quickly, more quickly than anyone he has ever met, and he will find it hard to resist the magnetic pull of her sexual attraction. Opposite signs are always attracted by the physical chemistry of the other sign immediately, and once an Aquarian man realises that this Leo lady is so different from him, he will want to know more, to test her out, see if she comes up to scratch.

Sexually, the Leo girl will find this man doubly attractive because he is so aloof. Cold men are a challenge, and she likes to prove her strength. But emotionally the Uranian man is an out-of-space man, and the chances that he will be able to fulfil her need for warmth, compliments and much admiration are slim. He may initially find this an amusing pastime, he does love his pastimes, but he will eventually tire of the game, as he tires of a worn out jumper, and revert to his social life. The Leo lady, whose pride is the mistletoe of her sexuality, can turn frigid very quickly, and look for a greater deal of comfort and warmth.

AQUARIUS WOMAN – LEO MAN

The girl who breaks all the rules will seem a prey of a delectable new species to be tasted by a Lion. Her unpredictable nature, her rather strange, analytical approach to life, are things that get the Lion's mane slightly ruffled when he first meets her. He is used to women who listen to him with very open ears and nods a lot, which makes him feel smug. Leos need to feel smug and this enhances his image of himself. This Aquarian girl won't ever make him feel smug, she's more likely to knock him over with her extraordinary, quite challenging rebellion. His Fiery emotions are vulnerable with this carefree and very independent spirit. She is not tamable, and he won't even dare try. She will find him quite vain, and wonder what he has got to feel so haughty about. His generosity will intrigue her and his enthusiasm for everything will actually provide the spark for her own inquisitive nature to burn. There is more to their emotional relationship than appears on the surface. The Aquarian stubbornness will resist any obvious signs of emotion, and the Leo will spend most of his time trying to impress her to avoid her ever really knowing how belittled he can feel in her company,

There will be times when her need to rise against the norms of society will infuriate him. Leos like to feel that they are above everybody, and that includes even a dissident Aquarian. Their sexual relationship can be passionate but often tainted by the Aquarian girl's coldness. Sex isn't a big thing for an Aquarian girl, but it is for a Leo. If he can understand that their friendship is more important than love, she can provide him with the sort of experiences in bed that are wildly entertaining, and certainly unconventional.

AQUARIUS MAN – VIRGO WOMAN

The first thing an Aquarius man must do is respect the fact that the Virgo girl he's become fascinated by is as independent as he is, but not interested in his friends. This may come as a shock to him, because he really dotes on his friends, more than he possibly would a dog. Why can't she just be another friend? Why does she insist on being someone special? Aquarians don't like to think anyone is more special in their life than themselves. Their friends, relatives, spouses, business partners share his equality rule. He will give pleasure to the world with the same amount of attention and will hope that those around him benefit from his ability to change them. The Virgo woman might not enjoy this at all. She can adapt to anything, with great ease, but she won't want to be changed for the sake of change. He will stubbornly exert his contrary opinions upon her most of the time, and she will attempt to remind herself that she saw in him a dreamer, a visionary who could make the world a better place. But he does keep trying so hard to be difficult and different. Turning a relationship upside down for the sake of it is the kind of tactic to alienate even a Virgo girl.

She is difficult to please, so there will be times when he

will slump off with his friends and ignore any conflict. He can get angry with her nit-picking and the way she has to clean up his chaos. He likes a rather obscure orderliness, one that he has designed. He will choose the most austere furniture, or the most way-out central heating system, refuse to have animals around because he gets allergic to dust and hairs, and stubbornly believes she would be a better woman for his cranky habits. If she can resist criticising his friends and accept that she will never be the only woman in his unorthodox life, then he might just agree to try eating toast in the morning instead of a piece of lettuce.

AQUARIUS WOMAN – VIRGO MAN

The Virgo man is essentially a loner and the Aquarian girl is mostly everybody's friend. She needs people around as if they are part of her very being. However, the Virgo man who has taken a keen interest in her extraordinary and unpredictable behaviour might be able to understand her humanitarian and extrovert nature. Aquarian girls like analysing and subjecting people to bold and frank inquiry. It's interesting for her to see how they tick, and whether they get upset by her form of character analysis. Funnily enough, the Virgo man can get quite happy on criticism and analysis too, but on a fussier level. Mentally they have much in common, but their differences can cause friction and tensions which may never get them further than a first encounter.

Being an Air sign makes the Aquarian girl fairly immune to emotion and also fairly uninterested in sex. She insists on maintaining an awful lot of freedom in her relationships, mostly so that her rebellious and lawless attitude is never subjected to restraint. The Virgo will attempt to let her have free rein, but he won't enjoy the company of friends in the kitchen, on the telephone, or hanging round their flat at all hours of the night. He has his routine and he has his order. She has no routine, the less routine the better, and she loves her chaos.

This can make them become either inextricably fascinated with each other or separate them quickly. Sex is not something either finds at the core of their lives, so if friendship and partnership are handled carefully they may stick it out. Not an exciting romance, but the chance of a lasting partnership.

AQUARIUS MAN – LIBRA WOMAN

The tactless and rather eccentric behaviour of the Aquarian man will usually make the Libran girl smile quite charmingly and ask questions later. She is nosy and would like to know why he is so fanatical about being different, and why he has to have so many friends. She loves people too, but she loves love as well, and the Aquarian seems to be about the coldest man she has met. His aloof and rather glamorous appeal will often at first seem a challenge to this quite strong and mentally fair girl. She will quite calmly seduce him, with her usual easy-going and apparent harmless charm.

The Aquarian will be naturally suspicious, will put on a cold confrontation to protect himself from her undoubtable attraction, and may even show her how territorial he is, either by planning her life before he's even got her to the bedroom, or by getting her to the bedroom before he even knows her name.

This touching girl won't be touched for long by his law-unto-himself behaviour and this is where they can suffer most in what could be a rather challenging and exciting relationship. What's fair to an Aquarian is not necessarily fair to a Libran girl. Actually she likes fairness, but it's the surface fairness, the closeness of it to her own life and love. The Aquarian will make generalisations, wrongly or rightly, and the only fairness to him is that the world should be a better place and everyone in it should be treated fairly. The

Libran girl hates conflict, hates ugliness in her own personal world, but the Aquarian would rather take on the whole of life and change it on behalf of change. He will love her loveliness, very much like his own idealistic truth. But she will find times when even their sexual compatibility, a rare thing for an Aquarian, will remind him that harmony is important in his own life, and the only way sometimes is perhaps to accept one person as more special than the rest.

AQUARIUS WOMAN – LIBRA MAN

The trouble with Air signs is that they need fresh mental inspiration for life's rather tousling affair with their jumbled heads. The Libran man could fall desperately in love with this rather mad and rebellious Air sign, and she could quite easily find that his fair and lovely charm will instil in her the right sort of Air that she needs to breathe. And the mental fencing that these two play in their relationship can be more fun than the Olympic Games. Libra is quite bossy when he wants to be and, once the initial infatuation has worn off, he might find he's tempted to goad the wilder side of the Aquarian girl's unpredictability into livening up the office party. She is incredibly stubborn and insists on being awkward just for the sake of it. She is more likely to have decided he was charming enough to be one of her friends to begin with rather than a lover. She is not usually the sort of female who goes around actively searching for a mate. The Aquarian female is in need of friends, friends and mostly friends! One day she will like the Libran's soft smile, and the next day she won't. She's not fickle like Gemini, she just wants to be different. The more unconventional and crazy she is, the more the Libran will be forced to admit he can't keep control. But he has to accept that the Uranus girl has to trust him first before she even thinks about letting him into her private life. If his romantic notions include sex (which is inevitable with a Libran), he might have to be prepared for some pretty cold nights warming up the bed alone, while she's out spreading the news about him and analysing his friends.

The Aquarian woman can be one of the most independent women of the zodiac. If the Libran man is forced to find solace in drink and women while she's trying to understand what happened to their friendship, he may come back to a lonely bed and a lonely heart. However cantankerous she appears, she won't tolerate infidelity, unless it's her own. He needs love and affection more than she does, and he needs to feel the solidarity of team spirit. She needs harmony in her life too, but it can be exhausting for a Libran man to have to be the Aquarian girl's friend rather than her lover: she can be too cold with his very special heart.

AQUARIUS MAN – SCORPIO WOMAN

The strong-willed and evasive nature of the Scorpio girl's emotional life is an instant hit with the Aquarian man. He is unconventional, eccentric, fascinated by the intellect, and prefers the company of disparate characters and oddballs to the normal beings that make up most of the population. (You may ask what star signs they are, and no doubt the whole of the 'normal' population is not necessarily made up only of the other eleven signs of the zodiac, but normal people can be Aquarians and not be aware of their eccentricities.)

Meanwhile, back down the romantic path, the Scorpio girl will have found a man who will seem as full of surprises as she is herself. She can hide behind a range of masks to suit her mood, but the Uranian man will have already analysed and poked deep enough to make his own judgments and theories, quickly concluded that she is vulnerable and tender, whether she cares to admit it or not. She usually won't.

If they get beyond the car door together he might have to remember that this woman needs sexual love with a big S.

Being friends, and she is capable at having male platonic friends, is one thing, but if a relationship that involves love is ever to get off the ground, then she needs to feel that passion is in his loins as well as in his head full of ideas. Aquarians, being a bit intellectual, can give the impression that sex is very much in their loins. But they will play that game to suit whoever it is they are experimenting on at the time. Sometimes a Scorpio girl can get the wrong message from his body language, and yet know intuitively that his heart and loins are not involved. She is possessive. He wants to get out and meet as many weirdos, as many women, as many of anything, as he can. She likes her personal freedom too, but his contempt for society, and his need to change the world and leave himself out of it, can be a small hint that actually the Scorpio girl is no more special than the man on the bus, which is where she may leave without a word, and jump off, before he really gets to know her deepest secrets!

AQUARIUS WOMAN – SCORPIO MAN

The compelling antics of a Scorpio man in full attack and battle gear, ready to ride over any competitor and to win the object of his desire, can be daunting to the self-reliant and independent Aquarian girl. She might laugh at him initially, she does behave erratically and unpredictably, and then she may find him fascinating. How can anyone be so mysterious and yet so calculating about life? Scorpio by now will have already set his target high. The bigger the challenge, the longer it takes, the better. Yet he will be slightly confused by the Aquarian girl's very eccentric and determined sense of herself. It reminds him of his own personal integrity, but his is living life dangerously, it is being alive, and feeling every feeling intensely. The Aquarian's is about analysing life, changing it theoretically, and as awkwardly as she can. She may find him quite magnetic, a wonderful subject for dissection, mentally and even spiritually, and he, of course, will be thinking and feeling along very different lines, usually sexual ones.

It isn't that he wants to notch up another female spirit on his ouija board, but he does find the enigma of this very individual and proud woman a compelling challenge.

For all her inquisitions, the Aquarian girl only wants a sensible and intellectual equal, a companion who will be as willing to inspire change, to get on in life and look at it. Unfortunately, the possessive and emotional Scorpio will find it hard to bring out in her the depth of passion and strong sexual instinct that he lives for. She may seem cold when he is a living furnace of passion, she may seem contradictory when he wants to know where and who she is seeing. She needs friends, not lovers so much, and the Scorpio needs lovers rather than friends.

AQUARIUS MAN – SAGITTARIUS WOMAN

The inventions of the Uranian man are often better in his head than let out on unsuspecting females whom he, at times, uses as part of his experiments. He is a genius of eccentricity and unpredictability, but he is not awfully good at being the lover of most girls' dreams. Aquarians are mentally fascinating, and physically often aloof and glamorous, poised with a feral instinct. And yet the fumblings of the Aquarian man can sometimes seem as distant as his heart. To the Sagittarian girl this man seems ideal. She needs romance, yes, but she adores his brain, gets off on his distance, because it keeps away from her own, and is intrigued by his cranky ideas and rather blunt admission to knowing that life is what you make it. He has ideals, and so does she, but he breaks rules and makes rules and puts up with her ridiculous forays into freedom. For this reason she may seriously consider forming a romantic attachment to him, but the problem arises when she finds that the Aquarian prefers to keep friends as friends, rather than engage in any special and distracting love-affair.

If the Aquarian man realises that this is the sort of woman who can put up with his mad-professor behaviour and his stubborn need to change those around him, he may slip into the relationship for its originality. She seems able to accept that he wants no ties, and also that he can't consider her more special than anyone else. She's also headstrong, open and honest, and has the guts to go where she wants to go and not to ask permission. Finally she may find his coldness doesn't always turn the pillow to ice. He may live on a different planet, but he is inventive in bed, and he does do some quite ridiculous things to make her laugh. Could be an ideal relationship if she has the patience to get past the lengthy friendship stage!

AQUARIUS WOMAN – SAGITTARIUS MAN

The honesty between these two is probably what first draws them together into a comfortable but spirited rapport. The Archer needs an 'honest injun' in his life, and he also needs to feel that she, like him, is free, independent and not likely to crack up emotionally at the change of the wind. An Aquarian girl provides a mental accessory to the normal high octaves of the Sagittarian train of thought. He will change subjects within seconds, and she will give him the fuel and fire to deal with it. She loves talking about every subject under the sun, and they both share the same need to have friends and oddballs in their life first, and lovers second. Who needs lovers when you can have friends? The Archer is probably more romantic at the beginning of any relationship with an Aquarian girl, and probably more willing to express his real feelings, but the Aquarian girl is also in need of an idealist, and one who has the sense and courage to spread that idealism. She isn't possessive, but Aquarians, like Sagittarians, are sometimes jealous. She can be stubborn about doing things her way. But because he has no need to be dominated, nor to dominate, he can accept her as an equal. When she sets her mind to some crazy scheme and becomes coolly distant, he is able to shrug it off with his usual adaptable carelessness. He avoids conflict with her, and that is the answer to their success. Passion runs deep through the Archer's sexuality, and at times she may seem too light and Airy, too interested in reading the next section of her book, when he would rather be looning around the bedroom. But both want similar amounts of freedom: the Aquarian for her friends, and he for his ideals. Both are optimistic about life and the future, and this can be a highly successful and mutually beneficial relationship.

AQUARIUS MAN – CAPRICORN WOMAN

The relationship between an Aquarius and a Capricorn is better suited when the Goat is a woman. The Aquarian man will be quickly attracted to this rather shy, undemanding girl with the strength of a rock and the ability to support him in his wilder, eccentric moments. If he would rather be building a computer in his garage, or riding a bicycle backwards, the Goat girl will be quite determined that he should succeed, as long as her own ambitions are rewarded. Goats live in reality, not in the abstract world of the Aquarian. But she can tolerate his need for non-conformity, as long as it doesn't threaten her own conventional way of life. The Aquarian rather admires the realism of the Goat, but he will be frustrated by her need for commitment, and promises of faithfulness. He can hardly promise himself what he's doing tomorrow, let alone commit himself to a woman for the rest of his life. He needs friends, lots of freedom and he needs to form new partnerships so that none is ever more special than any other. This humanitarian aspect may make the Goat lady shudder.

He will admire her practical common sense, and her quiet ambitions. She has calm and strength, and she is not excessive in anything. Both will enjoy sex together as they don't like to make a fuss about it, and they don't believe it to be the total meaning of their life. The Aquarian can be more variable about sex than she, but she has the understanding to accept his rather unpredictable behaviour when he goes off to spend the night with the chickens to see if they *really* go to sleep. She needs affirmation of her trust, but the Aquarian isn't awfully good at reliable words of love. But he can and he will attempt any challenge, and that includes the Goat he first saw at the top of that mountain.

AQUARIUS WOMAN – CAPRICORN MAN

These two are like the washers on a tap that's started to leak: one fits perfectly and never goes wrong, usually the cold tap, the other constantly needs mending, drips as soon as you change it, and then suddenly breaks, and it's hot. The first washer is the Capricorn man, and the second is the Aquarian girl who, although a cold and aloof star sign, can also get very heated about the injustices of life. Capricorn man will be reasonable about life, as long as he's in charge, and as long as it stays down-to-earth and tangible. The Aquarian girl will prefer the theory, the abstract qualities that make life work, and why we wonder why. This will seem nonsense to the taciturn Goat who will find her individuality too far removed from reality. He neither cares about why the universe began nor if there is a God, as long as it all works, and he's succeeding in where he wants to go. What is the point of skidding around trying to upset the balance, or telling the world it's going to end? The Uranian girl is not conservative-minded, she rebels for the sake of rebellion, and will incite total anarchy against the Goat and his conventional ways. One possible chance for this strange relationship is that they both have a very strong sense of integrity. If she can reasonably (which is part of her Airy nature) accept that the Goat needs to be shown that someone cares, then he may be able to communicate his feelings better. In the end the compromises will probably be hers alone. The Goat is rigid and unmovable, even though he admires her sense of purpose. This could be a very successful partnership, for a business-like marriage, but romantic love doesn't have much place here. They are not passionate by nature, her attitude to sex is detached and his is a basic instinct which he draws on as a reminder of power.

Aquarius

OCTOBER 1994

Your personal independence and freedom from constraint is one of the most important things that anyone must come to terms with when they become your friend. You have an aloof and almost glamorous air that is immediately attractive to new acquaintances and, because you are also unshockable, and prefer to look for the weird and wonderful people, you tend to make close friends with people who are very different from normal! The Sun in Libra until the 23rd may enable you to see that the more you expand your horizons and the more people you meet, the less you might have to search for the truth. The intrinsic value of any scheme attracts your probing and analytical mind, and yet you seek to find the differences and the bizarre within a situation or a relationship, and to set it apart from convention. The more abstruse and the more diffident or rebellious a person is, the more inclined you are to dig deeper and treat them as if you were Frankenstein and they were the monster!

The desire to be different for the sake of being different can have adverse effects on your friendships and love life. You love people, and need friends, and yet the paradox is that you want to be private and very individual, and the closer anyone gets to you, the less likely are you to make any commitment. The Full Moon on the 19th enables you

78

to analyse your own powers of communication, which are powerful, very open-minded and without judgment. In fact the more obscure or strange a friend is, the more inclined you are to probe and to become fascinated for as long as it takes you to find out what makes them tick!

A humanitarian at heart, you believe that everyone has equal right to your company, and whether they are of a different sex doesn't actually matter that much to you. Unfortunately close partners, unless they understand that your love is genuinely shared without commitment, can find this difficult to accept. You are not a flirt, merely an observer of human nature, and the more progressive your own intellectual life is, the more inclined you are to believe that your mind can always take over when feelings may dare to enter your heart!

This month with Mars entering Leo on the 5th you may begin to feel more channelled towards the lighter side of life and, with a beneficial aspect between the Moon and Jupiter on the 7th, you should begin to set straight your frank and open-minded manner through the vivacious and sometimes very inventive way that your friends love so much.

∿

NOVEMBER 1994

You are often renowned for being everybody's friend and, although you base love on friendship, rather than just sex, your apparent passion for some new romance or an interest in a new acquaintance can often be mistaken for flirtation or falling in love. The chances are you are more interested and fascinated in finding out that person's secrets and opinions to see if they are out of line and therefore acceptable. Yet you always do so quite openly, and shocking other people with your tactless questions and inventive lifestyle stops many of those you consider your friends from ever disclosing your secrets. They are without doubt withheld for the very reason that your emotions are kept hidden behind closed doors: the fear of losing your erratic and eccentric freedom! By the 22nd, you may begin to feel that your pals are beginning to rally round you again, after a brief period of your feeling neglected. Although you are often insensitive to other people's feelings, and can seem cold in the face of emotional truth, you must have the attention and mental equality and honesty of your friends. The Full Moon on the 18th puts your home and family life into focus. Although you have no desire to possess or to be possessed, you can appear easy and sociable at any family occasion and, with the best will in the world, you will always manage to maintain your individuality and your personal freedom from any restrictions that they may try to impose. Being friends with your family is more important than anything else, and it is often how you manage to keep an easy and light atmosphere in any dealings with relatives and their more intense family affairs.

A brief but luminous aspect between the Moon and Mars on the 10th reminds you that even you can experience feelings that rise to the surface and need to be reassessed. Falling in love is not a sudden infatuation process for you most of the time and, although you can feel the spark of physical attraction occasionally, you are never consciously looking for it. Friendships are the most important focus in your life after yourself and what you need in a partner is genuine affection and a partnership that is equal both mentally and intellectually.

DECEMBER 1994

December looks like providing a varied social calendar. You love social events of any kind, especially if it involves organised gatherings, where people meet with ideas, and opinions, and express new schemes or plans for the future. Although you love to instil change in your playmates' opinions and to see those close to you progress and deliberately veer away from convention, you often find that you cannot move out of your own rather rigid moral code. Seeing reform and expansion in others is fine, and you genuinely believe that everyone should do their own thing, but that also includes yourself and, ironically, doing your own thing is often being very stubborn and very fixed in your opinions! On the 2nd an important aspect between Jupiter and Pluto emphasises that you must realign your attitudes and feelings towards your image, and attempt not only to iron out any creases of error that you may portray to recent acquaintances, but also to look further afield for the truth, and still maintain your distance and remain uninvolved. But a heady social Christmas period could put a temporary hold on any deeper intellectual problems and you may enjoy, with your usual gregarious and vivacious abandon, the delights of friends and informal fun. The Full Moon on the 18th in the area of your chart relating to pleasures and romance might even encourage a light and enjoyable meeting with someone who puts more than a little physical desire and romance into your head! With the end of the year in sight, and your sexuality and determination for life full of energy, you might at last begin to see that the higher ideals that you aim for are without question within each and every person that you meet. This Christmas you might meet a few oddballs, but they are the ones who will make it special for you and, whatever their bizarre motives, you always know where your own ideals and materialistic truths lie!

♒

JANUARY 1995

A convivial and radical atmosphere inspires you often to delve deeper into others' hearts that should be best left alone. Your ability to unravel mysteries without giving much of yourself away can either enlighten others or make them embittered by your impersonal and seemingly indifferent approach to their feelings. Yet you know that your cold exterior hides a warmer heart. The amiable mental beginnings of any relationship is what matters but, if someone starts getting too intense and emotional for you, then the chances are you'll be out of the door. Your ruler Uranus is still currently in Capricorn and it makes a dynamic and powerful aspect with the Sun on the 17th. Together they could add a new dimension to a relationship or, more ominously, make or break any relationship that may be floundering or be in trouble. This period of the month could be crucial as a fine aspect between Venus and Jupiter on the 14th in the area of your chart relating to friends and your social activities might enable you to open your eyes and realise that the pleasures of life and the breadth of your vision are about to advance. You can at least relax and feel more philosophical about life and the enjoyment of your social whirls. Perhaps the taunting Sun and Uranus could only serve to sever or to change one partnership that was in need of reform, and reform is your one and only commitment! With Venus spending the month in the social area of your chart, you should at least be gregarious and full of energy, even if it means a different approach, or an inventive way of looking at an old situation. New perspectives are the way you can begin to idealise and analyse love and life.

♒

FEBRUARY 1995

After the possible tensions of early January you may begin to feel ready to direct your energies to more intellectual or mental pursuits. Insisting that you are right can often have an antagonising effect on your close friends or partners and, as much as you enjoy an argument or a few moments of hard conviction and stubborn resistance to opinion, you genuinely do not want to instil bad feelings, or cause emotional distress, especially within yourself. Being impersonal and robotic about life often means you can avoid deep feelings, because deep feelings involve commitments and possession. With so much regard for your own freedom and for others, this month you may find yourself torn between wanting to move in closer and unravel an intriguing romantic attachment, or steering well clear of it in case it means you get pinned down! Asking point blank questions may keep you amused for as long as the romance lasts but, once you know the wider implications of any relationship, unless it has a firm basis in friendship, you would prefer not to move into any deeper tangle. The powerful aspect between Mars and the Sun around the 11th and 12th might just put your desire for intrigue up to challenge your desire for pure and humanitarian love. But with Mercury in Aquarius all month you should have more versatility and more lucrative reasons to handle any communication with romantic attachments. The Full Moon on the 15th ensures that whatever form of altruism you may have begun to envisage as a romantic involvement, it looks likely to set sail on a longer course than you imagined!

♒

MARCH 1995

Being tied down to dates and being pinned down to promises is something you would rather avoid even with your closest friends or partners. It is often just sheer obstinacy that makes you prefer not to let someone know what you are up to, and this can often cause a great deal of jealousy and suspicion. Although you are always totally innocent in what harm you do, as far as you are concerned it can have serious repercussions if you don't occasionally bend a little with the flow. It is at times like these when your apparent outgoing and friendly easy nature can actually be your worst enemy. For the air you exude of casual and rather conceited indifference can upset friends rather than endear them to you. Eccentricity is one thing, and is attractive and valuable, but your insensitivity and personal freedom are valued too highly for you ever to feel genuine compassion. Your ideals are very high, and so are your standards, and when the Sun makes a powerful aspect to Saturn on the 5th, this can only enable you to take a hold on your attitudes and see whether your belief in your ideals and your intellectual aspirations should begin to include some commitment to those very friends you rely on. With Venus making an awkward aspect to Mars on the 14th, you may, for once, be swept off your feet and someone else's indiscretion might be on the cards. Your usual moral conduct is not without flaws, however, and although you can feel intensely guilty about anything illicit, you might do well to remember that you have physical and emotional needs too, for all your space-age and new age thinking! But your fascination for someone new as always can only last as long as there is intrigue, and maybe now you can restore your faith in your ability to remain friends and keep your own mystery shatterproof for as long as you want! You are not normally forward, but are always willing for others to take the initiative and suggest a firmer and more romantic relationship because you cannot resist a mentally exciting challenge.

The end of the month sees you back in some sort of progressive frame of mind about romance, and you may find that with the Moon making two gentle aspects to Venus on the 28th and to your ruler Uranus on the 25th that you can at least feel able to enjoy the unpredictability and unconventional love life that you choose to follow.

♒

APRIL 1995

Being the catalyst for the liberation of hearts from feelings of torment is perhaps what you most aspire to, and yet you quite stubbornly refuse to liberate yourself. The unconventionality and often rebellious methods you choose are intellectually expressed, and you may go to weird parties, or strange get-togethers or deliberately dissident events! As much as you love to see the world changing, hopefully for the better, there is little that will change deep within your own heart. The 1st sees your ruler Uranus at long last entering its own most treasured home and sign, Aquarius, albeit only a temporary visit. With such renewed vigour both increasing your own energy and motivating your ego into action, originality and eclecticism could even infect your love life and your close friends. This month you could begin to feel that the only way forward is to be even more quirky and eccentric than you have recently been! The Full Moon in Libra on the 15th can only emphasise your need for individualism, and finding it the further afield you travel or the broader you widen your intellectual vision, the wiser and more able you will be to realise your ambitions. If love is for everyone, then you and you alone can give it, without offering it to one person considered more special than the others. To love and to be impersonal about it is your challenge, and to be detached also means that you never have to suffer the emotions and heartaches of real humanity! There are those who may still seek to be classified as the one and only in your life, and if you find that giving more of yourself than you expected is directing you on the wrong course, then now is the time to revert to your altruistic nature and let them know about it!

♒

MAY 1995

Love is really what makes the world go round, and Aquarians are everybody's friend, particularly when they are feeling loved themselves. The less neglected you are the more able you are to share yourself, even though you may still seem cold and often aloof, for all your charming weirdo humour. Your anarchist wit and often wild and seemingly absurd pranks and gags usually make you the centre of most of your fun gatherings. With close partners, you can lead them into situations and outrageous fun before they even know it! This month looks set to be one of those quite manic and fun-packed months, when romance may be in the air but, with it, the pledge of friendship, and the love of pleasure and new intellectual fascinations. With Mercury already entering Gemini on the 3rd, you may be ready to express and communicate those things you want to get out and do at the moment. When the Sun enters Gemini on the 21st, romance should most definitely be in the air, even if you are not immediately aware of it. Love can creep up slowly around you. Although you can quite easily play the romantic – a glamorous concoction of icy feeling and careless egotism – you are not often aware that love may be staring you in the face! You always take your time in forming relationships, and putting off the sexual side of romance gives you a chance to scrutinise the opposition and decide whether they have anything at all to offer! A positive aspect between the Sun and your ruler Uranus on the 22nd adds a new dynamism and idealistic hope for the future, and may enlighten any relationship that is new and different. The more original the better, the more of a mystery, the more likely will it sustain your interest. With Mars entering the area of your chart relating to your sexuality on the 26th, you should at last feel that if you are drawn by more than friendship, then any physical love can now be shared and expressed in your usual vivacious style.

JUNE 1995

Your verve for style and originality shine at the forefront of your love and social life this month. Always known for your exciting, outgoing and friendly nature, you draw strangers as well as close friends to your attractive and apparently irrepressible manner. But as much as you find yourself surrounded by those with as many differing and unusual interests as possible, you are always slightly cold and will distance yourself as soon as anyone appears to be getting too close. Your need for independence means that any close relationship, or anyone who attempts to get a commitment out of you, must return the favour and ensure that you always have your freedom and your friends. This can be the cause of difficult relationships you have had in the past. The recent social whirl you have been experiencing should, however, continue for the rest of the month and, although your ruler returns to Capricorn on the 9th, the Full Moon on the 13th signifies a great deal of getting out and about with those cranky friends. Venus also puts her warm glow into Gemini on the 11th to set any romance on course for an inventive and original future in your hands! The strings of commitment, however gently they are pulled by anyone you may find fascinating as a friend, let alone a full-blown lover, can be the most cut-and-dried rope dangling on the end of a broken heart! With a powerful aspect between Mars and Venus on the 21st you may find that you are forced into a commitment that you cannot make, and you may have to act thoughtlessly and without sensitivity to avoid getting involved in anything that looks like a conventional trap.

♒

JULY 1995

This looks like being a month when you have to turn your attention to your relationships with very close and intimate friends or partners. The Full Moon on the 12th might make you introspective for a few days, but your usual ability to handle your emotions may expose them to your own internal examination. This space-probe should quickly clear up any feelings and doubts you may have about romantic matters, although, once any serious emotional conflict is past, you may feel free enough again this month to return to the scene of the crime just to check out what you missed, and you will do so only with impersonal and bare emotion. Finding out what you missed is really just a way of analysing *why* you missed the dangerous clues of obligation or anything that obvious in the first place!

With routines and work put behind you, the summer should now swing into action as the Sun enters Leo on the

23rd and you begin to experience an even pace with your friends. Mind over matter is what counts and, if you can instil these ideals into your close partners this month, you could realise that you're on the road to reform and progress for the benefit of others. A gentle and active aspect between the Moon and Mercury on the 27th reminds you that expressing your mood for change can also be the way forward, rather than just putting your hopes in others seeing the light.

However hard you analyse people to scrutinise whether they are suitable for your purposes, you do not care what they actually think, and therefore often pull the wool over your own eyes, believing you are broadminded when, in fact, you have just shrugged your shoulders and given their ideals and moral values hardly a mention in your head or heart. Friends can find this excruciatingly conceited, and you may discover that their apparent cranky behaviour is only a result of your actual insensitivity! But with Venus now entering Leo on the 30th, you should at least have time for intimate friends and this month should close with your ability to create a happy atmosphere where everyone is equal.

AUGUST 1995

Affable and observant you are, but you can also be tactless and your mouth blurts out truths that others may not be ready or able to hear without their feelings being crunched. This month close partners may begin to make more demands on your rational and inquiring mind than usual and, although you would prefer to avoid conflict within your close circle of friends, it looks like your unthinking and rather indecisive attempt at patching up other people's troubles might be taken as a serious slight against them.

Friendship is the basis of love to you rather than sex. And this month as the sun enters Virgo on the 23rd, and with a new Moon on the 26th, you may find that you are more sexually involved with a partner than you normally admit. However you could feel more comfortable even in your dispassionate moments and, if you try to communicate your deep need for affection and love, however cold and distant you appear, you may be warmly rewarded.

The Full Moon on the 10th highlights your need for personal freedom in everything you do, and it may put a strain on partners who might have thought more of you as a possession, than a freedom-loving individual. However, with the wonderful conjunction between the Moon and Jupiter on the 5th, in the area of your chart related to social occasions and your dynamic and eccentric friends, any clouds of tension may lift as you expand and progress your attitudes into your social circle with your usual verve and radical insight!

♒

SEPTEMBER 1995

Theorising about life is one thing, but putting those theories into practice is another! Where you often make mistakes in convincing others of your ideals and reformist cohesion is that you may intellectualise about the world and expect change, but you actually do very little about it yourself. Being true to yourself means keeping your liberal attitude wide open but, within your own structure, you are fixed, often to the point of pig-headedness, and as determined as ever! The urge to be different is your stubborn resolve that you *will* be different, and thus you never seem actually to put these changes into any real practice. Once the theory has been postulated, the experiment seems merely a waste of time! The Full Moon on the 9th considers those attitudes and opinions of others and the way you are drawn to dismissing them as instantly as they are expressed. Your indifference to a close partner may only result from a fear of any deeper emotions surfacing, and your nervous anxiety is then subject to attack like an open wound! You could also experience the restriction that you prefer to avoid this month, as Venus makes a rather condescending aspect to Saturn and both sex and your personal attitudes seem at odds, forced into a corner by a close friend or loved one. Having to show your hand is not one of your qualities, and cold withdrawal to another experiment or experience might mean you appear cynical about any of love's greater challenges.

But Mars now in Scorpio energises your ambitions and your image of yourself, and you know with certainty that in whatever ambition you endeavour, and with however much passion you face the hard reality of the world, it is by bloodless analysis that you can reveal the truth, even from the bottom of your own heart.

♒

OCTOBER 1995

However much you value your personal freedom, once you have committed yourself to someone, for whatever reason, and usually there will be a reason behind it rather than any emotional content, you have the strength and conviction to be loyal and faithful, even within the wide and liberal context of your relationships with both men and women. Often known to enjoy the company of the opposite sex just as much as your own, you can appear dynamic, glamorous and quite vivacious, and ready to involve yourself in any dark and illicit affair of the heart. But actually, in the pure and uncluttered light of day, you know that this is far from the truth. Not only is involvement in anything that puts your heart at risk or that might exclude your own closest friends, against your highest principles, you also know that friendship is more important than any physical twinge of desire. Mental stimulation and the freedom it gives you from your emotions is always preferable to tying up your guts in angry knots!

Mars adds verve and drive to a stony Pluto on the 20th and you should begin to see where your ambitions with regard to your relationships really lie. As Mars drives on into Sagittarius, and the area of your chart related to aspirations with friends and your very busy social circle, you should find new energy and determination to get things moving again. Any progress is better than none, and if things get static in your social life you'll certainly be the first to set it on a progressive course again. Even if it involves re-forming groups, having strange parties, and generally being as obscure and pseudo-anything as you possibly can! A good month for channelling your intellectual energy into your friends and to receive the return their constant respect for your blunt and forthright expression when, at times, you can be ridiculously tactless! With Uranus, your ruler, now moving forward you should feel that any nervous tension and any upsets of romantic or serious involvement are finally resolved.

NOVEMBER 1995

November sees your rationalising not only your relationship with a close friend, but also, perhaps, with the whole social scene that you love so dearly. This might be one of those months when the more original and inventive you are, and the more you can search for new attitudes that might suit your very odd view of the world, the more likely you are to be able to force progress and change around you. Both chances are with you, as the Sun makes an expressive aspect to Mercury on 23rd in Sagittarius and, along with two beneficial aspects from Venus to Mars on the 22nd, and to Jupiter on the 19th, you should be able and ready to pour that jug of life over your friends and your social life and inspire them with your glamour and high ideals. Being a cold front line means you often shrug off indifference with nonchalance, and any friend in need of support can rely on you this month to provide the chalice for their defence. Now with Pluto back in Sagittarius on the 10th, and the new Moon on the 22nd in favour of your expansive and eccentric endeavours, all social and intellectual activities look set to show you what friends are really for, apart from your own sometimes selfish amusement! These wonderful aspects can give you the power to show that your conceit is only a reaction against compromising your very deep need for freedom. But you are neither a snob nor an egoist, and would prefer that the world and everyone in it were treated with equality. However, your sometimes more anarchistic views on life can be put to the test, particularly your liking for bizarre and strange people this month, when you may be forced to choose between close and trusted friends and the lure of an eccentric and dissident lifestyle that entices your opinions to the forefront. There is more chance this month than any other this year, finally to meet the type of person with whom you can form a deep and positive bond. A partnership is not always your aim in life, and love, however you like to express it, is only part of deeper friendship. This month, with the number of social contacts you must make, you could surely do no better than enjoy a far-reaching and broadening relationship with someone very special.

♒

DECEMBER 1995

Scrutinising strangers and the intensity of analysis that you often make about people before deciding if they are suitable as friends, or even lovers, can often put restrictions on who has the tolerance to take such experimentation! With the Full Moon in Gemini on the 7th, you may have a chance for romance and an enjoyable, pleasurable December. When you get going and let your hair down, you are just as capable of doing the maddest and most outrageous things, and letting your witty and sparkling personality lighten your social life. Communicating your ideals and your rather obscure way of life to someone new and romantic might make the month pass more quickly than you had thought, after a gentle conjunction between Mercury and Jupiter on the 8th. Although the Sun and Saturn might blur the glamour for a few days around the 11th when someone else's grumpiness might put a temporary restraint on your freedom, you should be released from their inner tensions, once Venus conjuncts Uranus, your ruler, on the 20th, and at last you feel that you have at least got your relationships and your need for attention and affection in the right perspective, however hard it is for someone else to see your opinion.

Although you hate to feel neglected, there are periods when you need time to yourself to inspect whether your new attitudes are working against you. Contrary to everyone else's opinions, apart from your own, you can seem as if you are never satisfied. Alone and with only your own mind to play you can get lonely and, if Christmas comes and your social life isn't what you want it to be, there will be nothing to stop you getting back into the full swing of enjoying as many different people's company as you possibly can, and knowing that each has an equal share of the very deep and warm love that you have to offer the world.

Aquarius

BIRTHDAY PREDICTIONS FOR 1995

21st January – Unpredictable though you are, this year should see the change inspired by love from a perspective different from your own.

22nd January – Your fixed opinions may subtly be influenced by the vision of a new and lasting friendship this year.

23rd January – Broadening your outlook and meeting new friends is always easy, and this year you should find even more to fascinate you in bizarre encounters.

24th January – Friends play a huge part in your life this year, and you may find they rely on your loyalty more than ever before.

25th January – Without your social life, you would suffer severe intellectual frigidity! But this year you may have to give out more warmth than you care to admit.

26th January – You can feel confident that this year your progressive attitude to life will rub off on those you want to be your closest friends.

27th January – Independent and single-minded though you are, this year you can't do without the trust and stamina of your closest partners or friends.

28th January – Instead of inventing mind-games about your emotional relationships, invent a little more romance this year, and you could come out winning.

29th January – However ordinary you think your

relationship with someone is, you may be pleasantly surprised by a change of attitude this year.

30th January – No one can challenge your reformist and analytical mind, but be prepared for a confrontation in 1995, however faithful you are.

31st January – Your personal freedom may at last be accepted by someone very close to you, and it looks like a loyal and trusting relationship could gradually develop.

1st February – Communicate more about your feelings this year, and you should inspire the close confidence and love of a friend.

2nd February – Friends may find your self-expression less idealistic this year, but you should still find delight in changing visions.

3rd February – Try to be more understanding for 1995, and less insensitive, for someone special may hold the secret weapon to love.

4th February – A long-term relationship may have been suffering, but now it looks set to take on a new course, and with it new meaning.

5th February – Your attitudes to others may modulate your behaviour this year, and any eccentric notions you have about love can now be put into action.

6th February – Take time out this year to put more energy into your family and home life, and the original lifestyle you enjoy should thrive.

7th February – Self-sufficient as you are, you still need the support of close friends and relatives especially now you are about to take on new responsibilities.

8th February – Pleasure and romance might make you more extrovert than ever this year, and ensure a constant flow on new and sparky ideas.

9th February – Love can sometimes jump up at you from unexpected quarters, and this year it does exactly that. And don't you just adore the unexpected!

10th February – Romantic and idealistic progress should be made this year in all your social and pleasurable pursuits. Make the most of it.

11th February – You may have to keep on your toes, rather than observe from a detached position, as love tempts you from afar.

12th February – This year get down to basics and accept that a close partner is able to give you the freedom you need so much.

13th February – Mental harmony and a long-lasting rapport could be achieved this year, if you adopt a warmer outlook on your love life.

14th February – All emotional conflicts should be far from your heart, as someone makes an impact upon you that you cannot resist.

15th February – Love can be as unconventional as you want it to be and you now have the chance to renew an old and deep relationship or change your whole path through life.

16th February – There is more to your life than a happy sexual relationship, but this year you may be in for more physical fun than you anticipated.

17th February – However inventive your sex life this year, you must make time to let others know that you have a heart too.

18th February – Rash promises have a habit of coming back at you with heavier demands, but this year you might escape taking the plunge and thank your closest friends for their wisdom.

19th February – Insensitivity can only serve to establish where your true feelings lie this year, and where you stand with regard to any new emotional relationships.